Carly Simon

Biography

The Original Journey of an Artist and Author

Alexandra E Eersteling

CONTENT

Chapter 1: 133 West Eleventh Street

This could have been the day when my identity was formed. I hadn't given much thought to who I was before the tragedy. After that, I would spend the rest of my life putting myself to the test to see if I was correct.

After supper, the entire family met to meet a potential nurse for Peter, my brother, who had only been born five months previously. My two older sisters, Lucy and Joey, and I were all under the age of eight. On Eleventh Street, we resided on the top level of a six-story townhouse.

"Quick, girls, it's almost eight o'clock, the plane arrived an hour ago." Put on your shoes, stockings, and brush your hair." Mommy was smoking a cigarette with her lips. She tried to brush through the tangles in my feathery hair, and then grabbed a barrette, attempting to force my hair to go somewhere it wouldn't. She let it fall into a tangle of golden knots and moved on to a simpler task: brushing Lucy's hair.

Andrea Simon still needed to tidy up her chignon, put on her black calf heels, and apply a fresh coat of lipstick. She was always dressed in bright crimson.

I could hear Daddy playing the piano from at least three rooms away: a strong, beautiful classical tune he'd been working on. It sounded exactly like a vinyl record.

"I wish he'd play something from Carousel or South Pacific," Mommy expressed her request. "I believe it would make Mrs. Gaspard feel more at ease." "Rachmaninoff isn't for this kind of meeting," she says, as if any of her three little kids knew. She clearly meant it, for she gave us one last directive before sprinting into the living room to instruct Daddy, I guess, to stop playing what he was playing and play something more "fun." We girls followed her and could hear them having a brief quarrel before Daddy began playing "The Man I Love," from George Gershwin's Strike Up the Band. Gershwin had sent him a copy of the song. In 1948, my father was at the centre of the publishing world, and he had met Gershwin while the company was working on a book about him. Daddy founded Simon & Schuster with Max Schuster in 1924, and by 1948, things were only getting better.

"And he'll be big and strong, the man I love," Joey sang out loud. Daddy regarded his eldest daughter with approval. Mommy had gone to straighten her hair for a moment, and no one had noticed that I was not only barefoot, but also hadn't changed out of my nightgown. But it was almost as lovely as a dress. The nicest part was that Daddy had returned! He's reverted to his former self! He was back on top of the world.

The doorbell rang, and Mother, fresh from her and Daddy's bedroom, muttered in hushed tones, "Coming." She pushed open the large, massive front door, and a woman entered with the grace of a ballerina. She was tall, with an attractively square head and bright red, wispy hair. I was concerned that she would be overly strict. But because she was so tall and regal, we all came to the same conclusion: the potential nurse was auditioning for the position in the same manner that an actor would for a part in a play.

At almost three, I was the baby girl, a waif of blond sprouting from my scalp in opposing directions. My nose was larger at the bridge than both my sisters', which embarrassed my father, who, I later learned, preferred the Nordic look in the ladies he admired. My nose wasn't the only thing that let him down. After two girls, he'd hoped for a son, a male heir to be named Carl. When I was born, he and Mommy just added a y to the word to make it sound accusatory: Carly.

My uncle Peter had lately taken me to see Al Jolson's 1927 film The Jazz Singer. The only image that came to mind at that moment was of a man in blackface, folded down on one knee, arms extending. I jumped onto an adjacent coffee table without thinking. All eyes were on me as I went down onto one knee, my toes tucked under to position my weight and secure my balance, and extended both arms, waving my palms and yelled out a single happy, brassy: "HI!"

* * *

The town house at 133 West Eleventh Street, between Sixth and Seventh Avenue South in Greenwich Village, was my first home, the building where I spent my first six years during the winter season. My parents had joined the two top flats to create a sprawling penthouse on the six stories, each with two apartments. The decor, if any, was diverse, with rooms furnished in Simon-family Victoriana and books strewn across cases and shelves just large enough to hold them. Nothing fit or matched; everything was crammed together. The kids' rooms were separated by plywood partitions that didn't quite reach the ceiling, with single beds off a hallway lined on both sides with little slots for our shoes, sneakers, and boots. Dresses and coats dropped from small hangers suspended from a pole. It wasn't a problem of money, though my parents prided themselves on being frugal.

Chibie and Allie, our nanny and cook, who always made time for me, spent my early childhood with me. I'd show up at their third-floor apartment with a satchel full of shiny jewels plucked from my mother's jewellery box—her tourmaline engagement ring, pearls, and Jensen necklaces—and hand them over to Allie, who had far fewer bracelets, necklaces, and earrings than my mother did. I could tell there was a socioeconomic divide between Allie and our family. Still, why shouldn't Allie wear the same jewellery as Mommy? My Robin Hood-style jewellery-filching got so frequent that it became a sort of routine: I would pirate the jewellery to Allie, who would then lug it all back upstairs to my parents' apartment, and by dinnertime, my mother would be back wearing her pearls and rings, no fingers pointed, no damage done.

Uncle Peter and Uncle Dutch, who lived in the basement apartment, were my two favourite grownups, the ones who made me laugh the most. My first crush was Uncle Peter. During the summers in Stamford, Connecticut, I was his Robin Hood as well, slipping over the lawn at night and delivering desserts from my parents' fine dinner table to his little coffee-drip hut. Uncle Peter adored me just as much as I adored him. He made me laugh. He spoke in amusing tones. Behind everyone's backs, he made scrunchy faces. He executed a dance that reminded me of an eggbeater churning, with his torso whirling and rubber-boned as he made odd, ecstatic, spasming hand, leg, and facial movements. He also taught me to play the ukulele, which was where I learnt the antecedents to my first guitar chords.

I used to believe that every family in the world sang, harmonised, and played the piano together. Mr. Porter, the super who sang "Silent Night" all year, was one of half the residents of 133 West Eleventh Street. My mother had a lovely, delicate voice that I recognized from the Brahms lullabies she practically murmured to us as we slept.

Uncle Henry, my father's younger brother, came up with the idea of forming an orchestra and choir, with rehearsals taking place every Wednesday night at his clean, extremely beige apartment. Uncle Henry had gained his highbrow taste in prep school, in his case the Ethical Culture School in Manhattan, like the rest of the cultured, upper-middle-class, Upper West Simons—Daddy and his five siblings were all named after British kings. Our orchestra, at least as Uncle Henry saw it, would play only church hymns and liturgical songs. Everyone was pleased to perform together at first, even if Uncle Peter and Uncle Dutch would have preferred to play show tunes, blues, and jazz. Dutch could play a mean mouth bass, and Peter could play whatever Louis Armstrong could play, except instead of a cornet or trumpet, all the sounds came razzing, tooting, and overflowing directly from Uncle Peter's mouth.

Daddy's family was musically diverse. George, his younger brother, was a drummer who helped create Downbeat magazine. Alfie, another brother, was the program director at WQXR, a music radio station. Henry was a Shakespearean scholar as well as a classical music aficionado and conductor. Daddy, on the other hand, was the most gifted of them all, a nonprofessional pianist who could rival the experts.

As the youngest of the three Simon girls, I recall Daddy forcing me to leave the dinner table as punishment. I also recall kissing him goodbye and good night but never receiving much affection in return. "Darling, remember to kiss Carly, too," my mother said several times before bed, as if he may have forgotten about me if it hadn't been for her soft reminder and diplomacy. With Daddy at work, I resorted to my two slapstick-loving uncles, Peter and Dutch, during the day. They were my private Marx Brothers, making up songs the three of us sang together, teaching me risqué language, and taking me on double-decker bus rides up Fifth Avenue when my youth, and my family, appeared to last forever.

I used to think my father was a hero, a king, when I was a little child. Although I noticed his lack of interest in me, it made me think less of myself, not him. When I visited Simon & Schuster's offices in Rockefeller Center, I naturally imagined the massive bronze-cast statue of Atlas standing in front of their building was Daddy, carrying the celestial spheres on his shoulders. I'd enter the lobby and take the mirrored, gilt-edged elevator to the twenty-eighth level, where Louise, Daddy's executive assistant, would welcome me with a smile before escorting me down the hall to Daddy's office, giving me a ginger ale with a cherry and any snacks I desired. Midtown Manhattan was a mature, turbulent world, and my father was the most imposing man within it, just as he set the sophisticated tone for the cocktail parties and dinners Mommy and he hosted in New York, Stamford, or, for two or three weeks every August, Martha's Vineyard.

If Mommy seemed to idolise my father at the time, Daddy lavished her with affection while also admiring my two elder sisters, Joey and Lucy. I convinced myself early on that Lucy and Joey were Daddy's darlings, leaving me... who or what? The small child who'd greeted the new nanny with a big, barreling Hello? Joey and Lucy were both stunning as children, a pair of queens-in-waiting to my father's gorgeous chessboard king. They, too, were going places by the time they were in their late teens. Joey wanted to be a great opera singer, while Lucy wanted to pursue nursing (to which Chibie replied, "Uggh").

I aspired to be a pitcher, the first female pitcher to make it to the major leagues. I was a tomboy growing up, with irregular-length hair, a Dodgers baseball cap, trousers rolled up just below the knees, and punching my baseball mitt to break it in. Outside of my baseball fantasies, I had no notion where I was going, and my connection with Daddy was always distant and awkward for reasons I didn't fully grasp. I remember holding one hand in Daddy's and the other in Uncle Peter's on Father's Day when I was in kindergarten. Uncle Peter's hand felt and looked better to me. Why? I'm not sure. I only knew Daddy had smooth, dry, strange skin, as if he came from a foreign family or clan. After all, it was Peter who had taught me to play baseball, tennis, and, most importantly, music. If Daddy preferred Joey and Lucy, then Uncle Peter was mine, and I was his as well. I lavished attention on Peter whenever the opportunity arose. When he came off the tennis court in the summer, I offered him clean white towels, as well as milk shakes made of fresh strawberries and vanilla ice cream, with freshly selected four-leaf clovers on top. I never felt the same way for Daddy. When we were together, I felt a strange separation, but I realised that I was reflecting back what he felt for me. My inability to capture and hold Daddy's attention, as well as my suspicion that I was the least important of his four children, was a problem I'd spend my life questioning and compensating for. This is not an unusual circumstance.

Mommy and Daddy's marriage appeared iridescent from the outside, like a pearl under bright light, especially on nights when they put on a performance for an audience of dinner guests. Alone, once the guests went, they were never quite as dazzling. Daddy would grow professionally and personally, only to begin his slow-motion slide in the mid-1950s, when I was just ten years old. The rising part of Daddy's life, when he was a publishing entrepreneur, innovator, and magnate at ease with high society and the New York City intelligentsia, is mostly a legend to me, difficult to reconcile with the pained, remote, brittle father I remember much later, whose company and wife had both been wrested from him, and who roamed the floors of our house as if he were already a half-vanished man.

Chapter 2: Summer in the Trees

There was a summer, I believe 1951, when I spent a lot of time in the fruit trees in the orchard near our Stamford play barn, right beyond a huge copper beech tree. The orchard was peppered with apple trees, principally Cortlands, McIntoshes, and a few more unusual, difficult-to-identify species. There was also a pair of enormous cherry trees nearby, with longer trunks and bark that was darker, grayer, and harsher on your skin. Cherry trees were more difficult to climb than apple trees, with twistier turns, but the rewards were thrilling: spotting the first sweet, dark purple cherry, twisting off its stem, chomping around the pit, savouring the meat, and then—the best part—fingering the small wet stone like a bead and hurling it gleefully at a human target below. Then, with hardly a breath in between, biting into another, sometimes not as ripe as the first, and after a sour sample bite, tossing it with contempt toward the ground, or at the sister, brother, or cousin you'd missed the first time. I'd mastered the art and science of pit-marksmanship by the end of the summer.

When I wasn't preparing my lines, I sat on the grassy circle among the apple trees with Jeanie, pretending to talk to our imaginary pals, which included Mr. Hicks, Meany, and Bypress Fongton. The latter two settled on the pool house weathervane, while Mr. Hicks, who lacked a permanent residence, wandered between the orchard and the deep end of the pool, inciting conflict and causing problems for another of Jeanie's imaginary friends, Ha Ha Ginsberg, a character who became so famous for unknown reasons that her name appeared in a New Yorker story. When her father told her, Jeanie called upstairs, "Ha Ha, guess what, you were in The New Yorker!"

Our fictitious characters were us, and we were them; they gave us life, and we gave them desires and destinies in exchange. They fought off moths and bees, discovered prohibited gardens, judged singing, dancing, and somersaulting competitions, peered into family drawers, and ruled over acres of fruit trees that included the gigantic copper beech, sycamores, maples, and elms. We were the orchard's youngsters, the future Connecticut night actors. Fongton, Meany, and Ha Ha rang the mischievous bells as they coordinated their journey between the trees and the stars and back again, taking good care of us while we slept.

***

That was also the summer I began to withdraw from myself. I had always been a nervous, timid youngster. I was afraid of being alone, of the dark, and of Jack Frost's coming in the winter. Getting to sleep has always been a chore. Around 8 or 9 p.m., my mother or Allie would crowd around me at the bathroom sink as I washed my teeth and contemplated what to do about my hair. I was born with feathers instead of hair, which were so fluffy and difficult to brush that I often slept with braids secured with basic red rubber bands. Joey and Lucy were sick of the nightly theatre involving my hair—the twisting, turning, and yelling. Joey even set up a faux salon in my parents' bathroom a year later, and with Lucy as her accomplice, proceeded to scissor away all my hair with a pair of gigantic chicken shears. Joey just got the left part sliced off before I burst into sobs and rushed outside. My hair grew back after six months of uneven pigtails.

Getting to sleep was one issue, but sleeplessness was another. I used to make up crazy games in my thoughts to get myself to fall back asleep. One of my favourite fantasies involved a navy cruiser on a black, chilly, choppy sea. Life on board was a living hell, and it was my fate to share a bunk with a slew of other sailors—"me maties," as I dubbed them. I was a deckhand, although not as lowly as the others. My maties snored and sweated, spewed coughs, chokes, wheezes, and smoker's breath, had unclean feet and teeth, hairy legs and armpits, and snorted and sweated. They slipped and fell from side to

11

side, threatening to throw each other off the bow or gunwale—Drown, you nasty swab... no more vittles for you... you want your Frog Hog? That's all you've got.

As I worked on board, scrubbing the bathrooms and decks, I would give myself another inch of space on my own bed—a blanket edge, a pillow corner. Excellent swab! I cried out to the boat's admiral, who came by on a regular basis to inspect things, and every time I heard those encouraging words, I drew in a few more inches of bedding.

When the admiral concluded his inspection rounds, more and more of the bed and pillow would be mine and safe again. "Thank you, Lord," I'd say before praying for Mommy and Daddy, Lucy, Joey, Peter, and Allie. Chibie, Uncle Peter, and Uncle Dutch would also be on my list. Then I'd pull my blanket up to cover my miserable, salty, cold body, picturing a party and an imaginary back rub from the admiral, who looked exactly like Clark Gable as Rhett Butler.

I remember climbing my beloved cherry tree a week before our first, and I believe only the performance of Little Women, past my normal safe crook, was higher than I was supposed to go. My arms and legs came across a brittle branch beyond which no new branches or fruit sprouted. Beyond me was nothing but sky. Half of me hoped I'd lose my footing and fall, breaking both of my legs. Or, more dramatically, that I would shatter every bone in my body and end up in a full-body cast, unable to portray Amy or anybody else, much alone myself. My body cast would show the world that I had a visible handicap that I couldn't change, which would be easier than the bottled, twisted one in the back of my mouth that I was somehow responsible for. My primary concern was: Do I have any say in this? When you stutter and become aware of it, you stutter much more.

Backstage on opening night, before the curtain lifted, I heard whispers: "What if Carly stutters?" Should we just get rid of her? Should she have someone finish her sentence for her? Although my stutter was new, nothing humiliates stutterers more than having their words or sentences completed for them. We don't want to draw attention to ourselves. Overhearing the backstage murmurs, I only heard one thing: I had a horrific abnormality that had to be covered over, shushed, camouflaged, and lived out in secret from now on. Fortunately, a calf had been cast in Little Women that night to play—well—a calf, and when Jeanie took it onstage with a rope tied around its cute little head, the calf proceeded to urinate on the improvised stage curtain while emitting a particularly noisy little cow Moooooo. The laughter from the crowd entirely drowned out my opening sentence, "I don't think it's fair that some children get so many presents while others get nothing at all." I don't remember the remainder of the play, but afterward, I raced back into my bedroom and screamed until my mother returned. She couldn't say anything, but she hugged and soothed me.

If words and life had been easy and boundless up until that time, my stammer made me realise that life could also be difficult. There was very little about me that it would not touch. All of my future phobias drew energy and nerve endings from this item that I knew so little about at the time. Lines were thickening between neurons, generating pathways that became deeper and deeper, becoming increasingly connected with humiliation and low self-esteem. I waited for the stammer to appear, which it almost always did. I had no clue that during the next decade, throughout my grammar and high school years in Riverdale, and then for two years in college, I would endure the daily struggle to talk spontaneously or unconsciously. I was typically unsuccessful. Throughout elementary school, various students would brutally harass me, either to my face or behind my back, not only for my stammer, but also for the facial contortions and grimaces that accompanied it. Inside, I felt attacked, damaged, and devoured by self-hatred.

I'd return home from school, crawl into my mother's arms, and scream for hours. Friends had advised her on possible stuttering treatments. We never attempted the one that included filling your mouth with marbles and chatting. My stutter, however, built a relationship between Mommy and me beginning with Little Women. She was the only one who understood the guilt I was experiencing, which was beginning to define me. I cuddled in her lap almost every day, practising my words while she rocked and calmed me. She also applied a hot water bottle to my morning stomach aches—"your worry lump," Mommy nicknamed the aching spot—which made swallowing so difficult that I almost gagged. But every now and again, a word would get past my throat guards, undetected, like a prison break. "See, darling, you're capable!"'My victory was hers,' ' my mother would remark, and I felt it. But as soon as her enthusiasm for me wore off, my fearfulness would return. I had achieved something. Would I be able to repeat it?

My stutter followed no rules or patterns and continues to do so. On certain days, I could readily say a word beginning with a vowel, such as August or owl, but I couldn't say comb or garden. I could manage an s-word like store or Sunday on other days, but a t-word like train or toothpaste defeated me. The next day, without notice, it was flipped, with the t-words being easy and the s-words being terrified. He was always difficult. If the phone rang, I couldn't even say "Hello," so, like many stutterers, I devised accents, tactics, or techniques to deal with difficult words in unconventional ways. One tactic required holding my breath as the phone rang and answering it with a breathless "... ello?""On other days, I answered the phone with assurance, as if I were cupping a strong, queenly S in my throat, and delivered a regal "Simon residence." No doubt this must have sounded absurd, but it gave me a little sense of pride. Still, I spent every night wondering about the next day and the various reasons I could make: I needed to wipe my nose; I wanted to go to the restroom; I had a sudden episode of hiccups. My greatest fear was that my stammer would destroy my "timing," and thus any narrative I could be telling, or that if I answered a quiz or a problem, everyone would believe I didn't know the answer in the first place.

When I was approximately seven years old, I began keeping a diary, with most of the entries detailing what I'd eaten for dinner that night. To deal with my stammer in school, I developed my own code language over time. I once wrote, "Please—I pray that when I have to read aloud in class, I won't have a family." Famul: a word I made up that meant "stutter," designed to obscure its true meaning in case a stranger discovered the worn leather-backed journal I'd taken to hiding under my mattress, a word helpfully defined in a back-of-the-diary glossary. I couldn't envision anyone heading directly for the glossary, simply interpreting what I meant, locked inside my own apartness. What mattered was that concealing had become my game, and finding had become my shame.

My boyfriend, Nick Delbanco, told me when I was a teenager that he liked my stammer. Nick and I were sitting in the front seat of his Impala convertible alongside a lake in Larchmont, New York, late at night. Nick was a freshman at Harvard, and I was a senior at Riverdale Country School for Girls. It wasn't the first time I'd met Nick's parents, and I immediately felt comfortable with them. Through trial and error had helped to enhance my voice over the years, Nick's mother had sensed something was off. Had she seen it before?

Getting along with your boyfriend's parents is difficult enough without having to disguise your stammer. This evening was intimate, and inquiries were directed at me. I paused a lot, trying to conceal my facial contortions. I had no idea that Barbara Delbanco, a ferociously intelligent, dark-haired German mother who had raised three wonderful small sons, would be examining me from the line of my stockings to the silences between my statements on this night. Mrs. Delbanco was completely focused on me that night. Though none of the three Delbanco sons ever disappointed their parents—all became prominent in their fields as physicians, scholars, and, in Nick's case, prolific writers—Nick was, in my opinion, his mother's Buddha baby, the lovely, intelligent son who could do no wrong.

That night at dinner, I employed all of my stammering shortcuts and tricks: word swaps, glancing away during a facial contortion, letting Nick answer questions meant for me. I spit forth the worst of myself once or twice: eyes blazing up into my head as I battled over a phrase, locked mouth, clenched lips. Mrs. Delbanco took note of those few seconds. When I got back downstairs, I was so embarrassed by my performance that night that I told everyone I had to go home and write a paper, neatly cutting short the evening with an excuse that made me sound scholarly and responsible at the same time.

Tears began to fall down my cheeks. "I'm aware that I stammer. I'm completely humiliated. I'm truly sorry—"

Nick refused to let me continue. "Stop," he ordered. "I'm sure you do. That was something I noticed about you the first time we met."

The concept frightened me. He was aware, but why hadn't he said anything? "How come you didn't tell me that?"" I said.

"Because I loved it, that's why."

I couldn't even say "stammers" without stammering. "But … but … b—"

"It's seductive. It's a part of who you are. "I love you because of your stammer, not despite it." After a long time, after I straightened up, drying my moist face with my sleeve, Nick reached for me and just held me there, securely. "Carly, it's sexy," he said again. "It's also charming."

What an unusual concept. I'd spent the last ten years doing everything I could to hide my disability. In an instant, my stammer

16

had become charming and, even better, attractive. Nick Delbanco, a confident, worldly, literate Harvard boy, had loved away the shame of my stuttering. It had only taken ten years for me to become unique, distinct, and in a good way.

These days, I stammer when I'm fatigued, nervous, or, more infrequently, for no apparent reason. I still can't tell a joke that involves "timing." When I read aloud, I sound slow and unconvincing, and I'm transported back to my childhood's old red barn, Little Women, and the stop-start fickleness of my own throat. I still remember and relish the night in Larchmont when a boy I admired told me he thought my stammer was adorable. But acceptance has enabled me to speak about it. When my children were little, I would make up stories for them in the dark at night, and they appeared to enjoy them regardless of how I sounded.

* * *

Tennis and swimming were my refuges throughout the summer of Little Women and the debut of my stammer. Every day, I spent hours in the water, wearing my small bathing hat, practising my swan dives and jackknifes. Swimming, and the freedom I felt in the water, reminded me of how I imagined my voice would soon be: smooth, flowing, and without bounds. My stutter would emerge the moment I remembered I stuttered. Still, something else happened that summer that altered my life. My family and I were at the dinner table one night when I tried to say "Pass the butter." For some reason, I forgot to change pass to ass or "send the butter over." My stammer became frantic, and as usual, Joey or Lucy helpfully finished my sentence for me, a gesture that made me all the more aware of my speech handicap.

Then Mommy gave me an idea that would change the course of my life. "Carly, darling—try singing it."

Unsurprisingly, I couldn't at first. It was too odd, and the shift was too difficult. Instead, I sat back in my chair, tired. Joey and Lucy tried to cheer me up by singing "Pass the butter" to any tune they could think of, but it only made me feel worse. My younger brother Peter laughed at me, which made me feel better.

"Try tapping your foot," Mommy said, and I did, halfheartedly at first, then more vigorously. "Try saying 'Pass the butter,' but as if you were singing it," she said. Pretend it's a note."

With a steady 4/4 beat, I started beating my thigh. I had an instinctual capacity to recite the syllables offbeat, on a 4/4 syncopation. The outcome even caused it to swing. It was an easy step from there to add a little melody—C, B flat, E flat—at which point the entire table, including Sula, our cook, joined in, becoming a lovely choir grooving to "Pass the Butter." We utilised the table and the crockery as percussion. It became a habit that we fell into even when we weren't stuttering.

It was a release, yet it was tinged with the faintest, most cutting-edge of shame. Finally, I got a technique that worked, but I also thought, Oh my God, I need a technique. Even yet, I'll never forget that moment. It was a watershed moment. I now discovered a technique of dealing with my stammer, at least at home. Naturally, I couldn't sing what I wanted to say at school, a friend's house, or inside a department store, but did it really matter? Inside my head, there was suddenly a tune. It was beneficial to me. Not completely—there were years ahead of me, countless D's, T's, and S's to face—but I'd just been handed a critical new piece of ordnance. Instead, I could sing it. Maybe I'd be a good singer!

Chapter 3: Meet Ronny, Carly

I began losing my parents in the mid-1950s, around the same time Billy was gradually stealing a part of me. Mommy and Daddy were still present, but in other forms. Love, as I'd previously defined it, took on darker, more clandestine meanings and mysterious shapes. Our home became a hub of mystery, connotations, and late-night taboos.

Until that point, I'd been happily suspended in a Little Golden Books world, with their sunny, skinny spines and images of family normalcy—Daddy coming home from work; Mommy turning around from the stove, where she was placing the top crust onto the apple pie; Laurie the dog wagging her tail. I didn't realise how lonely each of my parents must have felt behind what appeared to the outside world to be an outstanding marriage, to the point where my mother began a connection with a much younger guy in 1954.

To be sure, I didn't know much at the time. Not until 1960, in fact. But the connection lingered in the air so strongly that I intuitively knew something was wrong, that my parents weren't in love, that what my sisters had told me was true: that when Mommy and Daddy kissed, it was all for show. Then I repulsed that thought and forgot about it. I used to ask Daddy to bend Mommy down as if in a swoon and kiss her with "passion" when I was a kid, possibly inspired by a romantic movie I'd just seen. When they agreed, their lips met uncomfortably, like two antiques clanging together in the back of a moving truck. In retrospect, I realised there was a reason I was constantly studying Mommy and Daddy for indications, hints, and clues about what was really going on in their marriage, attempting to read between the lines while rejecting everything that didn't fit into my storybook vision.

Why was Mommy so taken with this man, and why did she bring him into our home? What were they in common? I could only speculate. Mommy grew up poor in a row of red-brick-poached houses in the Germantown section of Philadelphia. Cockroaches were everywhere, and utilities and rent went unpaid. Mommy was always proud of her scrappy upbringing. Even as Mrs. Simon, she was never a snobbish, prissy, uptown brat, with perfect table linen, silver spoons, or china. Mommy had done everything she could to impress Daddy and the social circles in which they moved throughout their marriage. She had endeavoured to appear as a woman of words, despite the fact that smart men rarely sought out brilliant women. Maybe she had enough flair, enough acted-out glamour, enough "putting it on," throwing her hair back, applying crimson lipstick, finding the "just so" word or story in between the dessert course and the after-dinner brandies. Perhaps she felt bored, unappreciated, and unwanted. What she didn't realise was that the secret love she was about to start on within her husband's own home would deteriorate Daddy's health and likely prolong his death. Or perhaps she had suspected but had simply stopped caring.

***

Ronny's arrival in our life marked the end of my family's before and the beginning of our after. Mommy's seeming devotion to her husband and children began to fade as soon as she and Ronny grew attached. Her longtime job of being the outstanding hostess of two exquisite families, as well as the cheery, organised overseer of children, dogs, and various houseguests, had become foggy and messy. She appeared to be losing interest. She also drifted away from us in our private connection. The intimacy between us was shattered without notice. There was something new and strange about us. Our tenderness, which I'd always assumed was natural, appeared abruptly forced. For the first time ever, I felt self-conscious about our bodies making contact when we hugged, as if hugging her was some old, remembered ritual, and both of us were just going through the motions. It wasn't just that I was getting older and taller than her, but her hugs appeared to lack the customary warmth. Did Mommy realise, or suspect, that I was picking up on a new sexual current in her? I simply knew that I no longer ran to her lap every time I was terrified to go to school. Later, I'd understand it was Ronny who had kidnapped her, but all I knew at the time was that if Daddy was never mine, Mommy wasn't either.

Daddy withdrew into his work, his pain, and himself since he had no choice but to put up with what was going on in his own house in secret. His relationship with Ronny was always fleeting and strange. When they passed one other on the stairs, their gazes never met. Nonetheless, Ronny attended family lunches and dinners on a regular basis. He kept mostly to himself. When Daddy was around, he acted purposely servile—clearing the table, bringing away the garbage— but when Daddy wasn't, he acted like any other person at the dinner table. As for my younger brother, whose physical and academic development Ronny was meant to watch, Peter's responsibility from then on was to serve as Mommy's beard. They went to Coney Island at midday, went to nonexistent school picnics, and drove up to Stamford in the dead of winter to check on pipes that were completely OK and basement leaks that were not posing any immediate threats. Naturally, Mommy began spending significantly more time with Peter.

I began admitting everything to my diary, making up a fresh set of code terms to prevent anybody else from understanding what was actually going on in my life at school or with Billy, because I could no longer confide in Mommy and because my stutter prevented me from conversing easily. Stammer evolved from family into stanford, a term similar enough to Stamford, the town, that any astute trespasser would be perplexed. Ronny was Disk, and then Hark, the name of a strange individual from James Thurber's The Thirteen Clocks.

I scribbled my disdain and resentment of Ronny—"an intruder," I called him—on page after page. I wrote that he stank and that "I won't even tell you how much I hate him." I once wrote in code about the time Joey, Lucy, and I discovered Ronny eavesdropping on us in our restroom. We were combing our long hair and stroking our naked bodies with oils and lotions, posing as if for a French Impressionist painter, when Joey suddenly muttered, "Sshhh!" and tiptoed to the bathroom door, where she saw Ronny stooped, one eye looking through the door jamb crack. Joey swiftly exited the other bathroom door into Lucy's room and circled around, approaching Ronny from the opposite direction. Ronny pretended to be rehearsing a random football move, grunting an unconvincing "Hike!" as he dashed along the corridor without glancing back. This was quite entertaining, and we had no idea what to make of it. Then there was this diary entry: "Oh God, please make them happy, and please make Mommy love Daddy as much as Daddy loves her." Most importantly, please make Daddy pleased. Make Hark leave.``

None of my wishes were granted. Even so, it came as a big relief to me when, a year or so after moving into our house, Ronny was drafted into the army and stationed in Germany. By that point, I'd begun to act out around Ronny, to the point where I told him I hated him and invited my more tomboyish friends over to the house to gang up on him and punch him—often in the crotch—though, in retrospect, my behaviour was more misguided sexual attraction mixed with confused revulsion.

Our house appeared to exhale when Ronny left for Europe, not to return until at least the following summer. Life returned to a state of normalcy that I couldn't recall. Despite increasingly difficult days at the office, Daddy had Mommy to chat to when he got home from work at night. At night, the aromas of Daddy's favourite dishes wafted in, and Mommy appeared more attentive, sitting in the evenings and listening to him play the piano—and I may be mistaken, but I believe there were some smiling at each other.

As a result, Mommy's decision to travel to Europe in late October of the same year was shrouded in secrecy. She planned to travel alone, without Daddy. Of course, in retrospect, her vacation was all about Ronny. Mommy left for England by boat a few days before Halloween when I was ten. Daddy had his first heart attack ten days later. Mommy refused to return home even after she was informed that her husband had been sent to the hospital. Instead, Aunty Jo, a loving, zaftig Swiss woman who had raised Daddy and his siblings, stepped in, moving into the house for over two months to oversee Daddy's physical and psychological care. (She explained that he'd had a "muscle spasm," similar to the ones people have in their brows or eyelids.) Daddy went from home to the hospital multiple times, suffering from one tiny ministroke after another, the ambulance rushing and blinking up our Riverdale street in the middle of the night. Every day, Joey, Lucy, and I faced the possibility that Daddy would die, and then what? My heart shook every time the phone rang. Aunty Jo was always quick to reassure us that Daddy was gradually improving and that everything would be fine, but none of us believed her. How could she be certain? Why wasn't Mommy there to support him?

During her nearly two-month sojourn in Europe, I grew to despise some aspects of my mother, her absence a dark stain that persisted long after she returned home in mid-December and proceeded to cover the house with holly boughs for Christmas as if nothing had occurred. With Daddy going back and forth to the hospital, I'd developed a new nightly practice of tapping on wood exactly five hundred times before falling asleep—an obsessive superstition that, I reasoned, would save Daddy from dying.

When Mommy returned from Europe, Daddy, the third man in his marriage, did everything he could to demonstrate his forgiveness and to be a better spouse. Daddy felt well enough to travel to Europe on business in 1956, after recovering from his heart attack, and his letters home to my mother at the time were loaded with emotions like "I love you, my Cosa." Then there was this: "I propose... that both you and I forget completely any grievances we may have ever had against one another." We've both been living 'with our own blessedness of turmoil' (Wordsworth), and it's past time to leave that dead-end partnership. Because of my physical state, I am not permitted to perform the types of things that would make me the best spouse in the world. But I'll be able to do those things shortly. The best way to get started is to get started... Dick, I love you."

It wasn't until I read those letters later that I became engrossed in my mother's other, more secret-filled life; saw her for the first time from the perspective of my own life and years; and realised, as if I needed reminding, that what happens in a marriage can never be understood by anyone other than the people who live in it.

Still, my ten-year-old self was primarily relieved by Christmas 1955: Ronny was gone, out of the country, out of our lives. He wouldn't return for an eternity, and even if he did, my parents would have rekindled their love, Daddy would be fine, and Mommy would be everyone's Mommy again, especially mine. I wanted to believe that my parents were perfect.

Chapter 4: Splinter-Friendly Steps

The buoys were as obvious to me as if they had come from the radio next to my ear. It was exciting to return to the Vineyard. Each return was more exhilarating than the last. During the late 1940s and most of the 1950s, we rented or borrowed a house on the North Shore, a short walk from Menemsha's hamlet and beach. Joey was not always the only one who went up. Lucy and I shared a bedroom, clothes, and books of folk song chord sheets.

The Vineyard is notoriously beautiful, frequently compared to parts of Scotland and Ireland. Plots of land are casually separated by stone walls, like a phrase that does not take the route you expect it to go, but instead goes in a different direction. Sagging barns on ponds overlook meadows and marshes. The island flattens out on its south side as the interior ponds and streams reach the ocean. Turn around, and a trail or an inlet will lead you to a pier and a little rowboat with a single oar. Scruffy fishing boats almost vanish beneath the enormous coils of rope used to hoist pails and other traps that bring in lobsters from the depths.

Between 1938 and the late 1950s, when my father was less able to travel for a variety of health and business reasons, my parents spent practically every summer there. My mother was still in love with my father back in the good old days. And the sound that the buoys produced against the dock during the summer of 1956 was still the "Daddy and Mommy are in love" sound.

As far as I could tell, she still adored him. Mother admired her husband's aristocratic and romantic clout. In response to his typically dry humour, she produced a natural and appreciated throaty laugh. When his narrow but sparkling blue eyes locked on you, it was nearly too much to bear. His tan against his white shirt rolled up to his elbow, revealing just his Bulova watch, and his smile from the country of the leaders seemed to keep her satisfied. Mommy enjoyed entertaining in the Vineyard way. Just lobster or clams on the half shell, corn on the cob, baked potatoes boiled in seaweed in a trash can on the lawn or beach, and plain wine. humble neighbours (or expensive ones pretending to be humble) arrived for a sunset meal. They laughed and sang songs as they wobbled home under the stars.

The next morning, Lucy, my brother Peter, and I took a different route to the Menemsha market (Seward's) to grab The New York Times and muffins for breakfast. We walked down Dutcher Dock, then up a hill, past the five small residences perched on a bluff facing Vineyard Sound. Our parents had told us that the houses made up "Socialist Hill," because the leaders of labour organisations either met or resided there during the 1940s. All the stories about people who revolted against capitalism appeared incredibly romantic. Max Eastman, who had first introduced us to the island, had written about Trotsky, Lenin, and Stalin. He made them appear to be romantic outlaws. I couldn't imagine outlaws. What did they have to say? What were they wearing? Many years later, in the 1980s, I bought one of the five houses on the hill. For ten years, I prepared clam chowder while living with the ghosts of the Bolsheviks.

Lucy, Peter, and I were conscious that we were trespassing as we picked a few sprigs of this and that while strolling over Socialist Hill and watching the tender little waves as they lapped on the shore of Menemsha Beach. We mostly stuck to the walkway, and as we got closer to Seward's, I noticed a reflection of myself in a car window parked in front of the market. I was dressed in a white off-the-shoulder stretchy top that exposed my belly. My hair was medium length, half blond, half brown, half short, half long, and so a tangled, compromised mess, despite the fact that I'd acquired a tan in the previous three days. I stepped in front of my siblings, confident that I looked well enough to be seen.

As I was walking around the store porch, I noticed a very cute youngster who appeared to be a few years younger than myself. He was sitting on the porch steps with Davy Gude, another Vineyard child whose parents were friends with mine. Lucy spoke a casual "Hey" to Davy. Lucy and Davy had been the subjects of a series of images taken by Daddy of them holding hands as they went through fields of daisies. Lucy, poised and charming, had already been claimed by the class's youngest male deity, in this case Davy Gude, who was devastatingly good-looking even as a four-year-old kid, as early as kindergarten.

I bought what I needed for Mom and then handed Bill (Seward) a dime for a vanilla ice cream Popsicle, determining that Lucy could have half. As I walked away, the screen door crashed, sending a sound directly into the middle of Davy's note. He sang the word roll exactly in time with the door squeak. Jamie was now strumming the guitar. I gently drew down my white elastic top, which had ridden up my left shoulder. As I sat down on the step next to Jamie and took the paper from the Popsicle, they were all singing a chorus of "Roll On, Columbia, Roll On," including my little brother, who didn't know the song. I began to eat it. Jamie turned to the left, and there I was, seated right next to him. He was expertly playing the song's chords while hinting to me, with his long chin pointing in the direction of my ice cream, that a taste may be a good thing, but... he didn't even look at me. He simply took a nice bite off the top. Then there was another. He'd finished half the pop when he started singing with Davy again, without looking at me. He simply had excellent ice cream aim.

Billy was making me sick. These music gods, these magnificent tan boys singing and smiling, were my age. I almost had to leave the community centre because I was thinking about Billy. It was a horrible sensation. But I quickly forgot about it, and I came to think of it as something utterly "other." Perhaps it never happened. Wouldn't that be fantastic? I kept seeing Jamie riding his bike everywhere. I discovered the Taylors lived on South Road, close to

Stonewall Pond, where the ocean almost meets Menemsha Pond. Up-island.

My diary revealed that I wanted nothing more than for Davy Gude to fall in love with me before the summer was out, but that wasn't going to happen. Davy and Jessie were a real, live, lovely couple that summer. But Davy did a lot of good for me. He hauled out his second guitar one afternoon at his place. He showed Lucy and me a new strumming method for "Winkin', Blinkin' and Nod," Lucy's song based on a Eugene Field poem that Davy was going to record for a record label!!! Lucy and I started singing that fantastic song at my parents' events, and we eventually recorded it. It was our "starting point," as well as our "break."

In addition to learning a lot of music, listening to it, and listening to other people play and sing, I stumbled upon a book about the Greek gods at the property we rented that summer. I read about Orpheus and Eurydice for an hour. I relished every heartbreaking detail, such as how Orpheus, the wonderful musician and poet, falls madly in love with Eurydice. They fall in love while he strums his lyre and sings to her, and they eventually marry. Eurydice is bitten by a snake and dies in Orpheus' arms before falling to the Underworld. Orpheus chases her, desperate to bring her back, pleading with the Lord of the Underworld for help. Overwhelmed by the beauty and magic of Orpheus' singing and playing, Pluto decides to let Eurydice return to the earth's surface, but with one condition: Orpheus must not even look at her during their ascension. Not even once, not for a second. If he looks, Eurydice will vanish forever.

Orpheus agrees, but as the two of them make their way out of the Underworld, Orpheus loses faith when he sees the first welcoming light. Unsure whether Eurydice is still there, he turns behind him, and the lady he loves more than anything else in the world and knows he will love forever fades slowly backward into the murky, twilit nothingness of the Underworld. "The story isn't real, it's a myth," Daddy tried to soothe me. Was it? I pondered. Is it? Why did I feel so drawn to its power at such a young age?

The myth of Orpheus and Eurydice was all about everlasting love for me, the wind-and-water-swept romance, about a gorgeous musical god so in love with a woman that he couldn't bear not to glance back at her. It was about the cool, purifying air of music, whether it was my father's exhalations of relief and wrath coming from the piano while I slept in my bed at night, or the sounds of Davy Gude's guitar as I peered at the lost, mystical, beautiful expression on his face. Music drew me closer to the concept of God. Music provided me with the energy to revise, revive, regenerate, and reborn myself. It was a palliative, a sigh of relief. I've always known it would come to my aid, just as it had bandaged Daddy, bypassed my stammer, and reunited my families. Both of them: my biological family and the children I would someday bear. Orpheus was always in my sphere of influence.

Chapter 5: The Dinner Party

My parents were throwing a dinner party in honour of the renowned English publisher Victor Gollancz on July 28, 1956. Peter, who was too young, always got a pass, but Joey, Lucy, and I had to dress up—never forgetting Mommy's whispered instructions: no jeans, no bare feet, no sneakers, no nail polish, no hair in curlers (of course!), no hats, no tight dresses, and if we insisted on wearing makeup, only a little, because Daddy had recently yelled at Joey for overdoing it. In reality, he had referred to her as a trollop. She cried long and hard, which revealed what trollop may mean.

Joey and I shared a bedroom in the front. Our second-floor bathroom had a balcony with a view of the front lawn, giving us sneaky glances of the visitors as they drove in and around the circular driveway, a procession of Cadillacs, woodies, and Bel Airs. Every now and then, one of us would be lucky enough to observe a private moment—a kiss, or a front-seat argument—before the pair in question neatly reattached their dinner-party masks, that sneak spyglass-peek of passion or hatred all the more fascinating for having been glimpsed from our concealed aerie. A man's body was visible. Dickie Bauerfeld was the youngster who trimmed dead branches and plucked fruit from the trees. For him to be there so late in the day was unusual. We were all crushing on him. Or at the very least his shoulders. We'd look at him for five minutes straight at times, but I rarely saw his face.

That night began simply, with little clue of the surprise that would come at the end, filling my journal with page after page of coded entries over the next few months. After winning the coin toss, I took a shower before Joey. That year, my hair was shoulder length, and after eliminating the knots with a broad-tooth comb, I set about replicating Lucy and Joey's method of producing pin curls around the base, plus a few extra in the bangs, with the goal of achieving a Rita

Hayworth-style dip.

I sat under the hair dryer for twenty minutes, reading an Archie comic book, the machine so loud that I couldn't hear Joey beating on the door. I knew my own hair would likely unravel or frizz very quickly, but Seventeen magazine had given me a few insider's tips. I took out the pin curls and let them dance damply and loosely on my head before attempting to recreate Rita's hairstyle. I then got a scarf to cover everything while it dried. The hair. The hair was everything. When I heard the thumping, I let Joey in. Her face was flushed with rage. I apologised and we switched places.

I then applied makeup in front of the bedroom mirror. Joey and Lucy had been excellent teachers. Persian Melon lipstick was applied first, followed by a midcoat of Pink Innocence, and finally, the essential finale: Nude Spring Dance lip blender. My salty, moist, oily skin made the acne I was working so hard to hide look like a little volcano poised to explode, so I applied Clearasil over my breakouts, reapplying it every few minutes because it melted. Then, recalling a scene from Gone with the Wind, I had the wonderful notion of dusting those places with powder. I yelled out to Joey, asking if she had any talcum powder, but she was still irritated with me for taking so long in the bathroom and didn't respond.

I put on "Moonglow," my favourite song of the year, the captivating string parts buzzing and crackling through the speakers of my portable record player, pushing up the volume as high as it would go and dancing as Joey ignored my cries for talc. I swayed my hips and looked in the mirror, imagining what Davy and Jamie could have seen if they had followed my gaze.

I'd decided to wear the blue sleeveless dress Lucy had passed down to me earlier that day. To avoid disturbing the turban that was keeping the pin curls in place, I put it on feet first, carefully dragging it up, negotiating the arm holes, angling it into my body, coercing it into a strange, foreign shape. After two summers adhering to Lucy's body, it would always have her camber. When I stood up straight, instead of a bust, there were two puckers that appeared like I'd been pounded twice from the inside, by a baby's fists.

Joey discovered me with my back to her, stiff-shouldered, still trying to arrange Lucy's dress around my gangling, resistive body, when she finally opened the bathroom door, holding the talc. I couldn't take my eyes off Joey's chest, from which protruded an infuriatingly grown-up pair of what were then politely referred to as "bosoms," or, more alluringly, "breasts." They were Hallelujah breasts, looming from inside Joey's white slip, hovering just above the waterline, breasts that belonged to the conclusion of Beethoven's Ninth Symphony, and I couldn't have been more enthralled, nor despised her more.

My mother's voice rushed us from behind the bedroom door, yelling from the bottom of the stairs. We both exchanged a quick, anxious glance. "I know a trick," Joey remarked abruptly, her voice now tinged with compassion. She selected a pair of white cotton tennis socks from her sock drawer, balling them up in her palm and rolling them out as flat as she could. Joey rezipped my dress and we both looked at the results: two points of uneven, lumpy, linen shapes protruding out into the room, again like infants' hands punching from within.

Joey tried hard not to laugh, despite the fact that I was crying and convinced that nothing in my life would ever work again. But Joey had another plan. She tore a piece of tissue and spread it across the socks, pushing and mashing the sock-tissue mix farther against my chest. Even so, it's a dead giveaway. Mommy's voice was heard again, this time warning and urgent. I removed the two sad tiny white socks, defeated. Joey wrapped a scarf around my shoulders, which I would have to keep close to my body. Then the two of us strolled downstairs like women.

I sat for dinner between Jackie Robinson and Don Budge, the world's top tennis player at the time. Our family has a long relationship with the Robinsons. Jackie and his wife had lived with us while they were building their own home in Stamford, a few miles away. Daddy, Jackie, and I used to drive to Ebbets Field to attend home games of the Brooklyn Dodgers. In the dugout, I would sit on Pee Wee Reese's lap and was even dubbed the Dodgers mascot, with the team making a special jacket for me with DODGERS on the back and CARLY on the front. I was very proud of Jackie, and knowing him meant a lot to me. Jackie Junior, his son, was my brother Peter's best friend. Jackie even taught me how to bat left-handed, though it never stuck. I adored him. He had the nicest expression around the side of his mouth, as if he was thinking about what he was going to say before saying it.

Mommy looked elegant and lovely across from me at the crowded, intimate table. Her gardenia complemented the white stripe on her rigid black-and-white cotton dress, the two colours zigzagging diagonally across her bodice in stark contrast to her red lipstick. She had the potential to be a dancer. She danced as she passed the hors d'oeuvres, and her eyes danced throughout the majority of her brilliantly designed life. Who wouldn't have envied Andrea Simon and her marriage to one of the publishing world's reigning kings and innovators? Despite having experienced his first heart attack a year ago, Daddy was still making round trips to Europe, returning to the office with new books and fresh publishing ideas. In only one year, he published works by Henri Cartier-Bresson, William Whyte (author of The Organization Man), and our dinner guest Sloan Wilson.

It was uncomfortable to say that at the age of eleven, I had no idea what a publisher did. I pictured paper being put into vats where colours and dyes raced and swirled together, beside heaps of parchment paper that needed polishing to become smooth enough for small, monklike people wearing pom pom-adorned caps to write on. Eventually, miles of Scotch tape and string would be used to bind the completed books together. Even though it was silly to imagine I had thought it, it was as cosy and comforting to me as the ridiculous notion that Mommy and Daddy were in love. After all, ideas might be ludicrous and still be valid.

Today, I can't help but recall Jackie Robinson and Benny Goodman sharing a table that night: Jackie, the athlete who had broken the baseball colour line in 1947, and Benny, the musician who had been the first bandleader to integrate jazz 10 years earlier, during an era of segregation, by hiring pianist Teddy Wilson and guitarist Charlie Christian to play in his bands. A counterattack in America's ongoing war on race relations was developing, and I later felt proud to have been a part of such an "advanced" era, even though it was simply another Saturday night at my parents' house.

Uncle Peter had been patiently waiting his time, and now he looked over at Mommy. "Don't you remember when you sang 'Summertime' for George and Ira?" he remarked to Daddy, adding, "And you accompanied her?"

Mommy used her cloth handkerchief to cover her mouth. Of course she remembered; it was the most humiliating experience of her life. "There we were," Mommy explained, "George and Ira, sitting in front of Dick"—referring to Daddy—"as I sang 'Summertime,' because they'd never heard it sung in a woman's voice before." But what did he do after that? "Is that your father?" Mommy's gaze was drawn to Joey, Lucy, and me with both brows raised. "Your daddy stopped me halfway through the song and said, 'No, Andrea, that's not quite right, it goes like this—'" Mommy paused. "And then he sang it himself." Your father actually interrupted me to rectify a mistake on a note! I was about to leave the room, ashamed, when George stopped me and said softly, "My version might have been the better of the two melodies after all!"

And then, whether they understood the song or not, everyone at the table joined in, with Uncle Peter even kicking in the saxophone sound he liked creating with his mouth, Satchmo style. Uncle Peter's act elicited a yell from Benny Goodman.

Porgy, Bess, and Laurie, our three dogs, began barking as they crept out from beneath the dining room table and raced toward the kitchen. Have you ever had a doorbell ring and no one answered it? Was there anyone out there? I told the table I'd be right back and dashed through the pantry and into the kitchen, looking for any excuse to escape.

Someone was softly pounding on the rear door.

Sula, Bea, and Lena, the three ladies cooking in the kitchen that night, pondered aloud who it could be: Who would walk up at the back door so late at night? They put the coffee cups on the trays on hold. The dogs scrambled together, a mess of hair and tongues, excited. Then I heard Lena's quiet, astonished exclamation: "Well, well, my word. It's not possible. We didn't expect you. No, not yet."

A tall, attractive man in a tan army uniform stood on the porch, his brimmed hat angled at an angle, casting a shadow on his face. Ronny. I forgot to breathe in that moment when he locked his stare on me. I slid by everyone—the three women, the three dogs—into the back pantry, where the enormous freezer was, then up the tiny back stairs to the servants' quarters on tiptoe. I remained motionless and trembling.

How should I proceed? Should I return downstairs to the dining room and explain, as any mature hostess would, that Ronny had unexpectedly stopped by and could we draw up an additional chair at the dining table? In fact, Ronny was the last person I ever wanted to see again. I had assumed I wouldn't. I could hear the charged, adult hum of rising voices and laughing from the dining room. Ronny was still chatting with Lena and Sula in the kitchen, and all I could do as I stood on the steps was hope and pray that this was all a big mistake that could be undone with the push of a button, that Ronny would simply retrace his steps to a car that would whisk him back to the airport, which would whisk him back to the war. The glorious, wonderful conflict that had taken him away. I was repelled by the jagged remembrance of his ingrown toenail in his foot. I was curious if that nail was still there. Perhaps it was destroyed during the war....

That was not the case. Ronny had returned to our home and our lives three days later. My sentiments for Ronny had not changed, but I had assured my diary that I would keep them to myself this time. Looking back, it was almost as if I'd understood how attractive he'd become, that I couldn't put a name to what I was feeling, but I also knew how dangerous that emotion was to my own self-control. "He really is a sweet boy," I wrote once, "and not bad looking at all." I understood, as a child does, that Ronny and Mommy had just resumed where they had left off. I was also uncomfortably conscious of feeling jealous, because Ronny was more focused on Lucy and Joey than on me.

I had no notion what to do with my emotions since Ronny had penetrated our home: Feeling unwanted. I felt plainer and less desirable than my two bird-of-paradise sisters. Jealous of the attention Lucy and Joey received from Daddy, as well as from boy after male. Even upset by the prospect of Mommy glancing sideways at Ronny with a flirty smile. The Simon family's secrets, subversions, and dark spirits were all very real. Billy. My mother's name. Ronny. I sought liberation in music, in the promise of transcendence and the notion that the purity and innocence of a legendary god might save me from darkness. Music to dance to, sing to, play with Uncle Peter to, and listen to my father play. I recall reading about Orpheus. I began to desire to find him. To meet with him.

Chapter 6: The Twenty-Ninth Floor

Some things you notice early on, but there are no words for them. They're just pieces of a puzzle put together by other people doing things, thinking things, making decisions, forgetting things, and, of course, lying about things.

I'd never been able to put a name to my sentiments for my father in my entire life. I had spent my childhood yearning for his love but never receiving it. As time passed, I drifted away from him, lost myself in a sky filled with a variety of clouds. I'd never been excellent at any of the things I thought Daddy valued. I possessed no natural talents. I wasn't as lovely as my sisters and couldn't play the piano. I couldn't help but recall the night he penned in my signature book, Roses are red, Violets are pink, I love you with your wonderful large nose, and I've just had a drink. I wasn't even excellent at my nose, according to Daddy, despite my mother's warnings not to take what he wrote seriously.

There was more to it. I wasn't amused by his presence. I fumbled and stuttered, and then I sobbed about it. I learnt slowly in school and, other than swimming, I wasn't really athletic. When I was three or four, and Daddy was recovering from the nervous breakdown that followed Peter's birth—an expression popular at the time that indicated a person became so nervous that he fell down the stairs—Mommy asked if I wouldn't mind putting on my tutu and coming upstairs to dance for him. It was ineffective. Nothing appeared to work, and as usual, the tall man in the home, whose long legs I had inherited, didn't seem to want much to do with me. Instead, he ignored me. He appeared to be looking for something he'd lost, either Mommy or even his former self.

I'd look around for clues by observing the individuals around me. Clues for determining who to imitate, how to dress, how to speak, how to act, and how to dance. I'd spent my childhood feeling unworthy and unloved. I wanted nothing more than to be confident in myself, to believe that I was brilliant at anything. Instead, I was a scratchy bundle of nerves, a walking pile of needs and conflicts, shy, terrified, wounded, and frozen. But my drive to hide was matched by an equally intense want to be noticed, on top, sought, linked, asked, begged, adored, and admired.

Joey, Lucy, Peter, and I had grown accustomed to this new Daddy by the late 1950s, and knowing that his peculiar conduct would embarrass my friends, I stopped asking them over to the house. Fearing that Daddy would depart at any moment, I became afraid to love him, resulting in a perfect circle of mutual rejection. We watched baseball games on television instead of sitting down and chatting, him alongside me in his dressing robe, sighing, absently cracking his knuckles, his breath stinking of stale cigarette smoke. But instead of accepting his attention, I felt almost afraid of him, as if I were inhaling a musky, terrible presence known as "Daddy."

At the time, I had no idea what was going on with Daddy professionally, or how badly his morale and position inside his own firm were being undermined. Marshall Field III, the Chicago department store heir, purchased Simon & Schuster for $3 million in 1944, the equivalent of about $40 million today, with the understanding that if Field died, Dick Simon and Max Schuster would have first refused to repurchase their company. When Daddy died in 1956, both Max and the company's business manager, as well as the lawyer René Wormser, who lived in our building at 133 West Eleventh Street and was Daddy's greatest friend, advised him to cash out.

Daddy didn't want to, but it was two against one, and in the end, Max and Simon & Schuster's accountant, Leon Shimkin, won. Leon told him that Daddy's health was an ongoing concern, and that selling his stock would relieve him of a lot of stress. Their betrayal was exacerbated by subliminal threats that if my father did not sign his name to the buyout, he, Leon, would be obliged to publicly reveal my mother's ongoing connection with Ronny, and what a field day the press would have with that. René, if he truly was Daddy's best friend, would have informed everyone of the conflict of interest and recused himself, rather than encouraging Daddy to sell off all of his Simon & Schuster stock.

My father's life was slowly collapsing in four packs of smokes per day, cholesterol, a cheating wife, two dollops of whipped cream floating in his morning coffee, and double-dealing coworkers. Arteriosclerosis had muddled his wiring, reduced his attention span, and hampered his capacity to recall events that had occurred barely an hour before. It's no surprise he was so easily duped by his Simon & Schuster colleagues and even his own lawyer. Daddy was left out in the cold as a result of a sly decision made by a gang of pinstripe-clad double-crossers.

That summer, when I was fifteen, was the last time I considered myself a child. I took Daddy into the city one day in mid-June, dropped him off in front of the Atlas building, and spent the morning at Saks, where I was looking for a pair of low shoes. I was concerned about our height disparity after meeting Nick Delbanco for the first time. I was five foot ten on my bare feet, compared to Nick's five foot eight and a half, and I remembered Mommy always reminding me that men prefer little women, both robbing my self-worth and elevating her own, which is why I was looking for flats and low heels.

I returned to Daddy's office in the Atlas building at 630 Fifth Avenue, across from St. Patrick's Cathedral, with my new shoes in hand, where pigeons gathered and hovered over morsels of popcorn, breadcrumbs, and other strange summer goodies. I entered the foyer and boarded the elevator to the 28th floor. But Louise, my father's long-time secretary, wasn't there. Instead, a new receptionist informed me that Dick Simon's office had moved one flight up, to the twenty-ninth level. "It's a shame," she continued. "He's gone up to the twenty-ninth floor now, dear," she replied again when I inquired what she meant. He has a beautiful large office up there."

The twenty-ninth floor was less comfortable and less impressive than the one below it. When I got off the elevator, there was no secretary to greet me. Nobody offered me a cherry-flavoured ginger ale. When Daddy arrived, it was clear that the receptionist on the floor below had called to inform him that I was on my way up.

My mouth couldn't find a comfortable posture, so I nodded hastily. I was afraid we'd run across some personnel from the floor below. Is it going to be awkward? Would they want to stay away from Daddy? I resolved not to be one of them in the future; I would never, ever ignore my father. I put my hand into his large daddy one a few seconds later. He and I had become allies. The elevator doors opened on the 28th level. The ancient floor where he had reigned. He had been Atlas, supporting the heavens. Daddy's eyes brightened and he appeared as if he could still be the conqueror. With those crystal blue eyes, he pierced the backs of the skulls of the guys who had just called him "boss." They twisted their heads, mumbled nonsense, or gazed at the walls to avoid making eye contact with Richard L. Simon.

As I descended the exquisite marble stairwell into Grand Central Terminal from the tropical humid Forty-second Street afternoon, I clutched his arm through the triangle formed by his elbow and shoulder. I felt more like an aide or a nurse than his daughter. My other hand was clutching the shopping bag with the four-pack of steaks, which were encircled by freezing blue ice packs. He wore his jacket over one shoulder and carried his briefcase in his left hand.

We boarded the Stamford local and found seats in a compartment designated for four people. I stored the shopping bag in the overhead luggage bin and crossed my legs under my light blue flower-print dress with the voluminous skirt in an attempt to look ladylike.

Even the most outrageous events in the world can be ignored, filtered out, or wiped away. All you have to do is want them gone bad enough. Like the place behind Ronny's bureau, like Mommy going back and forth through that dark, airless hallway, a prisoner of love. What was Daddy going to do about it? Why hadn't he made Ronny leave the house? Obviously, my perspective had been clouded by a combination of wants and hopes, things I'd read about in books, things I'd seen in my friends' families and their parents' marriages, and chats with my cousin Jeanie, who was not only one of my closest friends but also a family member. In the years since, I've pondered the scenario, but the puzzle pieces have never fit. The one thing I knew for certain, the only thing I believed, as Mommy had often told me, was that sex and love were synonymous. They were indistinguishable. And I was getting increasingly sceptical that the numbers were correct.

For a time, Daddy rambled on. He talked about his new modest office at work and how hard he was trying to see the bright side of things. The train abruptly bent, and a multicoloured bead emerged on his brow. I was shocked to see that it was blood as I leaned in to wipe it away before it got into his eye. But where had he been bleeding? Then another drop of blood appeared, followed by another. "Hey, that man is bleeding from his head!" shouted a child across the aisle.

Daddy, alarmed, stroked his brow. We both looked up to see that the blood came from the melting steaks. I was overjoyed. I hurriedly removed the red-soaked shopping bag from the open shelf above Daddy's head, placing it wet side up on the seat next me. Dinner, I assumed, had been spoiled. The operative word is "spoiled." The meat. Today is the day. The thirtieth floor. My grandfather. It was his shirt. It's his universe. The sky had fallen from his grasp.

I wondered who would pick us up as we approached the Stamford train station. It was usually Mommy or Joey. Daddy collected his Italian leather manuscript bag, while I stood behind him, tenderly cradling the now-blood-drowned steak bag. It was difficult to keep the juice from soaking into everything. Daddy clutched the railing as we descended the stairs to the parking lot, where Mommy greeted us in her convertible Cadillac, top down. I informed her I'd brought dinner home in a quietly hysterical tone. The tension dissipated as Mommy burst out laughing, and the bleeding steak bag wound up in the nearest dumpster. Mommy gave Daddy a callous welcome-home kiss on the cheek as I climbed into the backseat.

Had Mommy heard anything about the encephalitis outbreak in New Jersey? Daddy was curious. No, she hadn't, but even if she had, what could she or anybody do about it? Daddy took a breather. "Get comfortable with the idea that there's a menace out there." He went on to say, "Don't worry, though, they're a long way away."

"That's right, they're all the way across the Hudson," Mommy remarked loudly enough to soothe me. They are unable to get over here."

"Yes," Daddy responded, "but they could always take the Holland Tunnel."

Mommy laughed, which made me feel better. Daddy could still make her laugh, even if she appeared to be resisting the need at times. Was Ronny capable of uttering things like that? No, he wasn't even near. If Ronny's presence signified the end of wit and fun in her life, why did Mommy continue to love him?

We passed poster after poster after poster for the Broadway production of Camelot, starring Richard Burton and Julie Andrews as King Arthur and Queen Guinevere, on our way home. They used to be like that, I thought.

I love you, Daddy, I thought from the backseat for the second time that day. Nobody will ever do you harm again. He'd sunk so quickly. He was a wreck, both physically and mentally. His wife had been having an affair right beneath his nose. His coworkers had betrayed him. He was incapacitated, unable to act or retaliate. Recently, he and Mommy were driving past the Fifty-ninth Street exit on their way to supper with friends in the city when Daddy had a vision that he was supposed to be onstage at Carnegie Hall at eight o'clock. He became so lost and upset that he started crying. Was this just Mother's story?

That night, long after I had gone to bed, the piano began to play again from downstairs, directly beneath my bedroom. Daddy's rage and loneliness, his love, all flowing together, casting up through the floorboards to my room.

* * *

A month later, on July 29, early in the morning, my mother and Joey woke me up at home. Mommy informed me that she had some bad news to share with me. Daddy had passed away the night before. Mommy's voice was solemn, and she couldn't determine whether she should reach down and touch me. Joey stood beside her, stone-faced, and the two of us avoided eye contact. Mommy then exited the room. I entered the green-tiled bathroom and sat for a long time on the tub's rim. It was just 6:30 a.m. Outside, it was already bright, sunny, and humid, with a breeze blowing in through the French doors. I wanted Mommy to scream and wrap her arms around me. Instead, life was whirling into spirit, just like that.

I knew this was significant. This unlike anything I'd ever experienced before. For years, the thought of Daddy dying had horrified me, and I'd done everything I could to keep it from happening. I felt nothing now that I was alone in the restroom. How was I expected to react? What should I have done? Was it expected of me to cry? Was Mommy upset? It was difficult to tell. Instead, I focused on something unimportant: how big would the garment I planned to knit be if I cast 38 stitches on my medium-wide knitting needles? Were my nails too short for the new pink manicure lacquer I'd purchased not long ago? Would my brother Peter even notice if Daddy was missing? I began to feel dizzy.

Joey came in a few moments later, bleary-eyed, and began brushing her teeth. Arleka, an Israeli singer who was boarding at our house that summer, informed us that Daddy had come into her room in the middle of the night complaining of chest symptoms. Daddy had knocked on the door of my mother's third-floor bedroom, but no one had replied. Mommy was most likely sleeping with Ronny in his bedroom. I scarcely knew Arleka, but she was the one who told Joey and me about my father's death.

That night, on my way to bed, I remember stepping somewhat sideways down the hallway, then slowly up the stairs. The walls were covered in images taken by Daddy throughout the years. Our dogs surround Mommy. Mommy posed once again beneath the Arc of Triomphe. Stamford's three Simon sisters by the pool. I'm at the top of a swing, getting ready to fall. I was tiny, and the grass was enormous.

Some believe he constructed his empire to amass wealth and glory.

If you ask him why, he'll tell you it's all for her, all for her, all for her.

He said hello to the little woman, and she said hello to the huge man.

—From "Hello, Big Man," 1983.

Except for that one train excursion that summer of 1960, the year he died, Daddy and I had never had the connection that my two elder sisters had. Nonetheless, Daddy left the most profound and long-lasting imprint on my personality. Our relationship may have been strained, but on a single train ride from New York to Stamford, I understood, as if for the first time, that I genuinely loved him, and I have to believe that he reciprocated. I felt as if I assimilated him into my identity as time passed, despite the fact that I only knew him as a sick guy. Many of my personal struggles, both good and bad, were similar to his: self-centeredness, humiliation, inadequacy, ambition—depression. The songs I'd create, the melodies I'd sing, were always accompanied by some image or notion of Daddy, one that seemed to be sealed inside me forever. Not only that, but whatever narrative I told in those songs constantly returned to the same themes: love and longing. Virtue. Crime. Secrecy. Vulnerability. Monsters. Beasts. The subway system. What happens when you walk through life bearing someone else's mantle?

Joey accompanied me upstairs. Bob, her boyfriend who had been a rock throughout the ordeal, had handled all of the funeral arrangements. Joey was in a guest room with Bob, but she kissed me good night, as did Lucy. That night was dreadful. Nothing was correct. I called Nick the next morning, and he agreed to come over the next day.

It appears that the world may be a very frigid place. My siblings, our twin Labradors, Porgy and Bess, and Laurie, my dog, were the only exceptions. I couldn't help but think back to a few summers ago, when I was unconcerned despite the presence of Billy and Ronny. My parents' dinner gatherings were like gold, gleaming beads strung on a necklace. Show people, and composers, fresh compositions booming through our house: What's the point of wondering whether the ending' is sad... You're his girl, and he's your guy... There's nothing else to say.

Chapter 7: The Mistral's Difficulties

It was 1961, and Daddy had been missing for just over a year. His ashes were dumped from a small plane over our Stamford property's copper beech tree. It was a difficult time between my junior and senior years, and I barely made it into college. Lucy was a student at Vermont's Bennington College, so I assumed I'd have a chance there, but Bennington put me on its waiting list. Joey had gone to Sarah Lawrence, so it seemed like a foregone conclusion, but Sarah Lawrence only accepted me as an "off-campus" day student.

The reasons why were not particularly surprising. I hadn't done as well as I could have in high school, owing primarily to my stammer, but I had a few undiscovered cognitive issues—a psychiatrist later told me my brain was like a crazy tossed salad. My speech impairment prevented me from engaging in most classroom discussions—just finessing the guttural r's in French class was nerve-racking—and when it was my turn to read aloud in my other classes, I would make any number of excuses why I couldn't. I felt a tickle in my throat, indigestion, and a horrible ache in my knee that required an immediate visit to the nurse. I would burst into frustrated tears instead, followed by even more excuses, like blaming my issues on allergies, because I was too embarrassed to disclose my condition with anyone. Of course, my stuttering continued to have an impact on my grades.

My SAT scores were similarly dismal. I cheated because I was so afraid of failing that I copied the marks of the girl sitting next to me. Unfortunately, her test was different from mine, therefore nearly all of my answers were incorrect. Midtest, I also had a panic attack, prompting me to flee to the bathroom, trailed by the proctor, whose high heels clacked against the gym floor, and into the girls' room, where I locked myself into the stall and sat frozen on the toilet seat, my head in my hands, my throat stopped up, my heart beating in my chest like a captured bird. I didn't return to finish. It was then arranged for me to retake the test at home, but my results were still insufficient to entice any self-respecting college admissions office.

I was still dating Nick Delbanco, and every swan I saw crossing the lawn, sitting in class, or waiting in line at the dining hall made me worry, If Nicky sees her, I'm screwed. But what else could I have anticipated as the daughter of parents whose actions raised more questions than answers about sex, love, and loyalty? As a girl who'd been introduced to male-female intimacy with Billy in the darkness of my family's pool house, it would have taken a miracle for me to start college with any confidence at all.

I didn't even have the dubious self-assurance that comes with money. No one at Sarah Lawrence thought I was a rich girl, and I'd never grown up feeling privileged, save for one or two occasions. At school in Riverdale, a group of my classmates was discussing who had the biggest house in town, and mine, I recall, was tied with another student's. Another occasion, the kids discovered that Daddy was the "Simon" of Simon & Schuster, whose name appears on the spine of a variety of library books. But, true to the Simon family's attitude, having money meant never talking about money, and in college, surrounded as I was by so many daughters of "name" families, I felt like the polar opposite of a big fish and lived comfortably on the twenty-five dollars a week Mommy put in my bank account. The huge secret was that not much of Daddy's money remained.

It was around this time that the dark force I'd come to know as the Beast began to form within me. It started when I started comparing myself to every girl I saw, always feeling "less than" them. My waist was too big for me. In dancing class, I wasn't as graceful as the other girls. In class, I couldn't read aloud. When I compared myself to other girls, my "not-good-enough" mentality became more powerful. I recall thinking, "This is some kind of Beast."

Nick and I met in the little Pennsylvania hamlet of Wind Gap, where Joey, Ronny, and I were performing in a summer stock production of Kiss Me, Kate. It was the conclusion of my junior year of high school, and I had gotten a summer job as a makeup artist at the same theatrical company that had offered Joey and Ronny starring roles. I knew how to put on mascara, but I have no idea how I ended up onstage as a butler, in blackface, singing "Another Op'nin', Another Show," or as the understudy for Bianca, the second female lead, whom I was given with the assurance that I could sing my dialogue if I couldn't speak it.

Nick drove to Pennsylvania to see me one night, and the spark of romance that both of us had felt before reached a new level. When Nick and I were canoeing on a lake one day, the energy between us passed back and forth. Nick and I took turns judging the desirability of the lake's weekend residences, earning silent points with each other while we slowly paddled. We were embracing a few minutes later, me standing below him on a gentle slope, making sure I was positioned so that we were around the same height. I was completely captivated. Hugging Nick was a lot sexier than I'd anticipated.

I eventually learned that I'd been initiated into sex numerous times throughout my life. I'd been exposed to it in some form or another since I was eight years old. Billy and Nora. Ronny and his mother. Timmy, a serious high school boyfriend with whom I practised the age-old ideas of first, second, and third base. But it was with Nick that I officially lost my virginity. Surprisingly, my deflowering occurred on the same cement bordering the swimming pool in Stamford where the majority of my summer encounters with Billy had occurred. I'm still not sure where to put Billy in my sex/love duet scenario.

Nick and I were walking about the Stamford property one starry night following my junior year of high school in mid-July. At Stoneybrook, I showed him all my favourite places, such as the red barn with the Ping-Pong table and the apple orchard, the windmill and the greenhouse, the tennis court and the pool house. We walked down the stone steps to the pool together. The night was warm, with a strong breeze. I was dressed in Bermuda shorts and a T-shirt, whereas Nick was dressed in khakis and a loose white linen shirt. I've always admired men with longish hair, and Nick had the proper head and nice looks to pull it off. His surname, Delbanco, indicated that he was Italian on his father's side. "A pure product of the Italian soil," Chibie said when they first met.

The moon made the air gleam, as if it had been polished. Nick grasped my hand in his. It was our first time together. I compensated for his awkwardness by moving like a gazelle (or so I believed at the time). He drew me closer till our bodies met, and then he kissed me on the lips. This was my love story. It's all mine. Nobody stepped in. There were no ghosts to be found. There are no recollections. It's just Nicky and me.

* * *

Just like in high school, I spent the first two semesters of Sarah Lawrence addressing professors' inquiries as infrequently as I could. I would hide out in the restroom throughout class, sometimes twice in the same class, to escape getting called on. Did my lecturers have any suspicions? Naturally, they did. I was the stuttering white elephant in the room, present or not.

I'd become a boarding student by my second semester, immersed in the complete Sarah Lawrence College experience.

I brought my guitar from home—one Lucy had helped me choose at Manny's Music, the famed instrument store on Forty-eighth Street—and concealed it under my bed once I started living in a dorm. For

49

the next few months, I practised my guitar whenever I could. Lucy and I both came home on weekends, and I remember intently observing her every step. I mimicked the things she wore and the songs she sang until I developed my own style. Lucy was impersonating Joan Baez at a period when her debut record was the dominant influence on an entire generation of females. Judy Collins, who was bold, blond, and blue-eyed, was another excellent newcomer to the music industry.

My sister and I hadn't started playing music together yet, but by the time she departed for Bennington, she was comfortable with the guitar and had purchased her first very decent one during her freshman year. She learnt just enough chords to play every song on Joan Baez's debut album. Her register was similar to Joan Baez's, a high, pure soprano with a heavy vibrato. I purchased my first guitar during my senior year of high school, and soon after, my friend Jessie Hoffman and I began writing and performing songs together. The title of the first one was a combination of our names, "Si-hoff Blues." Lucy would teach me chords on weekends and then over the summer, which fueled my desire to play and sing. I purchased a few records and began impersonating various singers. My voice didn't travel very far up the scale, but it was rich and resonant. Odetta was my musical heroine at the time. Her voice was everything a woman's voice could be: deep, resonant, and nearly demanding. I listened to her albums alone in my room at home on my poor little machine, whose needle scratched every LP I owned, tapping into my own lower register. I trained myself to manage my breathing in order to extend phrases with vowels like home and alone, stretching that o out comfortably in my lungs, hollowing out my throat and moulding my mouth into a long-columned O. I had a naturally powerful, even vibrato, and diverse locations with high ceilings and natural acoustics—like gyms, restrooms, or any tiled room—provided wonderful environments for me to learn to appreciate my own voice.

Simultaneously, Nick supplied camouflage. I sunk and hid beneath his eloquence, charisma, good looks, kindness, and the senior Sarah Lawrence girls' jealousy that I, not one of them, was hanging off his arm. I was obviously, and prematurely, in love. By making love in Nick's Harvard dorm room, we broke every norm. I was enchanted by the romantic poets of the time, and Nick was always quoting poetry to me, raising passion and sex to something otherworldly.

Outside the bedroom, Nick was equally seductive in his wide-leg, slouchy corduroys and handmade shoes, his long black hair falling in a gleaming blade over one eye. As a director at the Loeb Drama Center on Brattle Street—how Nick learned to direct plays like Lorca's Blood Wedding and Sartre's The Flies was a mystery to me—he dressed the part with long scarves and berets, a gentle, measured voice, and seductive, almond-shaped, dark brown eyes. I wondered if Nick was aware of the impression he made on others. My guess is that he anticipated it.

With my long earrings and pale pink lipstick, I was becoming recognized around Sarah Lawrence not just as a singer, but for the first time as a "hip" girl, a "in" girl—"cool," at least by mid-1960s standards. Nicky's father sent him an article on the French singer Françoise Hardy because he thought the two of us looked alike, and my friend Lani once told me gravely that she and I were the only two people on campus with "swank." It was a near relative of twirl, the term used to characterise my father's technique.

The Simon Sisters. Lucy and I both felt that our stage name was schlocky and somewhat embarrassing, and neither of us wanted to be labelled — or discarded — as just another novelty sister act. But in the summer of 1963, armed only with our guitars, we devised a plan to travel up to Provincetown, on Cape Cod's tip, and land a singing gig. As we drove from car to truck to car up and down the Cape, earning singing engagements left and right, we fantasise about being little-girl Woody Guthries. We were courageous and slightly decadent in this vision. Nothing more sophisticated than that—and we had no hopes of getting "discovered." It was more of a joke than anything else, a step up from singing at our mother's cocktail parties.

Lucy and I spent our first day in Provincetown walking the whole length of Commercial Street, the town's major thoroughfare. We stopped at every boardinghouse and tiny motel, seeking a room to rent because we didn't want to contact Mommy and say, "Help!" We'd been travelling all day and were both fatigued by the time we found a single, inexpensive "bug crawl" room (a euphemism for lodgings with a spider here, an ant there) above a noisy restaurant. With a sink in the bedroom and a public bathroom down the hall, our room felt small and tight.

Instead of practising, we went to the beach and decided to go for a swim. Something happened on the cold sand that, while insignificant in the grand scheme of things, I remember as a watershed event. I imagined Bert Lahr as the Cowardly Lion, both to impress Lucy and to put myself to the test. I was going all the way in, I assured Lucy, shaking my hands and yelling "Courage!" with Bert Lahr's overdone, burring "C-C-COURAGE!" I tramped ahead of Lucy into the frigid water with half-girl, half-lioness bravery. Lucy's cheers and laughing welcomed me as I turned around and rushed back to my towel on the sand, trembling. Even if I spent barely a millisecond in the water, I realised: you can always mimic yourself into something better. You can become someone "other," taking a vital step away from oneself, as I had done by singing over my stammer or answering the phone with an accent. Costumes, headphones, earbuds, blindfolds—all of these were steps away from the terrifying, agonised, naked self.

My sister and I immediately adjusted to our new B and B, dividing up sides of the bed (one, two, three: shoot) and taking turns in the shower after being refreshed and invigorated by being on the beach. We then unpacked, hung up our things, and chose the least wrinkled to wear. We dressed in similar white, full-sleeved Mexican shirts that were attractively pleated and fastened in at the waist by colourful woven belts; our full, generous, knee-length linen skirts were meant to be wrinkled anyway. Our slave sandals, which were fastened around our tanned ankles, reached all the way up to our calves. We were all about our tans and youthful, head-turning bodies that night, at least. Our hair was natural, wavy, and somewhat damp, and it was long and undone. Instead of worrying about how we looked, Lucy and I should have focused on learning a few new songs to add to our repertoire, but for some reason, neither of us was concerned.

Our voices together created an intriguing, nearly ideal blend: the exact same word pronunciation mixed with an entirely distinct vocal tone. Lucy's tone and delivery are more sharp, whereas mine are softer and more smouldering. She clarified my husk's point, and in the end, we sounded like a single voice. We sang a few more songs, including "Winkin', Blinkin' and Nod" (Lucy's soon-to-be-famous song), "Delilah's Dead and Gone," a Serbian folk song from the Theodore Bikel songbook that required five chords (Lucy and I knew four and a half), and two or three Harry Belafonte songs, "Day-O" being the undisputed crowd-pleaser.

* * *

I spent the remainder of the summer at Cambridge with Nicky, reassuring him about everything he worried would happen to me once I entered the big terrible world of show business. Nicky was horrified at the prospect, convinced that my new life would be filled with late hours and exposure to various seductions. Nick had introduced me to the intellectual world, and he was concerned that I would ride into a Sunset Boulevard world while losing a deeper, more thoughtful side. He had always insisted on me singing for the Harvard boys, but he would have loved to remain my personal impresario. Why would I want a larger audience when I already had him? I assured Nicky that the glamour of Hollywood would not transform me or make me love him any less, nor would I attract the

53

attention of all the Western world's playboys.

Despite Nick's concern about my head spinning in all ways, it was his head that turned first.

It occurred in August of that year. When Lucy and I returned from Provincetown, Nick and I leased a house in Menemsha, Martha's Vineyard's little fishing village. It was a one-room dwelling with multi paned windows all around, an outhouse, and a back-yard shower. A brook ran alongside the short road, and there was a walkway that meandered over a wooden bridge, past flowery plants, honeysuckle, and columbine. Nick was working for a local fish market, carrying bales of fish to various seafood stores and restaurants on the island, while I was relaxing and visiting friends. I could hear him typing at times, and at others, he and I played gin rummy on the pier. Nick was also teaching me how to play chess. Lucy had arrived in New York to begin a semester at Cornell Nursing School.

I drove back to our modest house on the pond one gorgeous afternoon after picking up the mail at the post office. I intended to spend an hour or two on the beach while Nick worked, then return home and make supper for him and my parents' lifelong friends, Max and Yvette Eastman. But first, I went through the day's mail. There wasn't much there: a bank statement and an overflowing envelope from a mutual acquaintance of Nick's and mine from Fieldston School, now a Radcliffe student. Despite the fact that the envelope was addressed to Nick, I opened it nevertheless because it was from a common friend. I shouldn't have done it. Our pal claimed to be serving as a go-between. The other, more crucial note in the envelope came from Nini. Nini wrote, "I can't bear to go around hiding our love in the shadows."

I sat on the bed and rested my elbows on the headboard. I was exhaling heavily. Fear had taken control of me. I was trembling.

Nicky and Nini's courtship, from what I could tell, had been going on since the spring. Then then, may I be misinterpreting things? In reality, being wrong was the only thing that could save me. The bubble of trust was abruptly shattered, replaced by a sense of utter invasion and hostility. I'd never considered whether Nick was disloyal to me; I just knew he was. When you know something, you don't have to believe it, as Jung once remarked. Jung, or I, was completely wrong.

When Nick returned to our broken-down cottage, he knew just where he wanted to go: my mother's rented house. I'd left my car in her driveway, and Nick, knowing me so well, knew I'd be at the beach. As I ripped the sand, I was already shifting emotionally from "me" to "her," as if I were a character in a story. Not me, Carly, fleeing, upset, navigating razor-edged rocks, but some unnamed her, jilted, deceived, and scorned, turning into a heroine in search of a sandy spot to collapse, drooping, sobbing, and moaning.

Nick had caught up to me. I couldn't fight him because I was out of breath. He rejected everything, saying, "No, no, no..." I couldn't do anything about her... It did not occur... You have to believe me! That person would never be me. I adore you. I adore you! Carly, Carly... it's not what it appears to be... I swear... And, like so many foolish, willful fools, I believed his story to be true—or, rather, my character did. In the movie storyline that was running through my thoughts, I desperately needed to keep Nicky and my status quo. I'd decided to be blind so many times before, a decision I'd have to make again and again for the rest of my life, in different forms and with other people. But that day on the Vineyard's shore, I told myself that I had to believe Nick, that Nini was insane, and that Nick didn't love or even like her all that much. I was curious how long Daddy had trusted Mommy.

* * *

55

During my time at Sarah Lawrence, I continued to commute to Greenwich Village, meeting Lucy in front of Cornell Nursing School on East 69th Street and taking a cab down to the Bitter End or the other club where we performed, the Gaslight. The Simon Sisters were the opening act for significant rising talents on the downtown comedy circuit such as Bill Cosby, Dick Cavett, Woody Allen, Johnny Carson, and Joan Rivers. We were two sisters who could harmonise like the Everly Brothers, complete with major-seventh chords tossed in for good measure. We stood motionless onstage in our identical outfits. The owner of the Bitter End, Fred Weintraub, introduced us—"The Angelic Voices of the Simon Sisters"—and then we'd break hesitantly into song.

Who doesn't respond positively to being loved by a large group of people? I was no different. All of my college buddies came down to watch us, and my mother and other family members were sometimes in the audience as well. People said I had a strong stage presence and sang naturally. Mommy adored our music, but she was often critical, saying things like, "Your voices weren't loud enough." The Simon Sisters typically performed brief sets of five songs, concluding with "Winkin', Blinkin', and Nod." We opened for some pretty outstanding performers, including the Tarriers, Judy Henske, Judy Collins, Randy Newman, and other solo and group folk musicians. When Woody Allen asked us to evaluate his nightly stand-up routines, we did so, delivering him actual notes! Lucy and I had begun to take ourselves seriously by this point.

I recall eagerly anticipating the release of the album. I met Lucy at nursing school, and we raced downtown together. First, we went to Harold Leventhal's office, where he informed us that the first album review had arrived, and it was genuinely positive. Then we dashed over to the Doubleday record store—there were three major record stores back then: Doubleday, Hudson Records, and Sam Goody's—and when we saw our record for the first time, Lucy and I jumped up and down and hugged each other. Then we walked into separate listening booths, put on headphones, took them off, screamed, and began bouncing up and down again. I couldn't have been more excited about the Simon Sisters' debut album (would Daddy be proud?). My joy was usually overtaken by apprehension about coming onstage and having to chat in between songs.

Odetta came to see us sing one night. Lucy and I were performing at the smaller of two venues within the Lenox Inn in western Massachusetts, with Odetta performing at the larger. We met after her performance, and she said, "Maybe I'll come see you tonight." It goes without saying that I worked myself up into a frenzy. When Lucy and I walked onstage that night, we were surprised to see Odetta seated in the front row, and I promptly lost control, fainting—quite literally—onto her table. When I awoke, Odetta was fanning me backstage, while I lay flat on the floor.

It took many shows and a lot of nice feedback for me to feel at ease. But with Lucy at my side, I knew that if dread overcame me, I could always count on her to come in and calm me down until the panic passed. I was less concerned about stammering onstage. I could introduce music and even tell anecdotes with an ease that always amazed me. I had no reason for my stop-start eloquence, and I recall thinking to myself that if I got stuck, I could always take a long break. My terror was also unpredictable. Lucy and I were singing in a college gymnasium one night when a bomb scare was called in, and I've never felt more tranquil or self-contained, or capable of reassuring others. That's not to claim that being onstage would be easy for the rest of my life. I was always on the edge of imploding, humiliating myself, and reawakening the Beast.

What came next was the question.

* * *

Nick and I boarded a train from London to Milan on a late February afternoon, when I purchased a rudimentary Phillips tape recorder the size of a shoebox. We were eventually on our way, driving blindly into France in Nick's new Alfa Romeo, up the winding, tiny roads of the Alpes-Maritimes, in France's extreme southeast corner. By the time we got to Châteauneuf de Grasse, it was so dark that I couldn't tell the stone from the stucco or the terra-cotta from an olive tree.

As Nick unpacked the car, I caught a glimpse of the distant lights of Cannes and relish the thought of seeing the Mediterranean in the morning. It was chilly, but it was a different type of cold, with a moist, throaty wind coming in from unknown hills and waterways. The trees whistled in French, sssss, a single note modulating and cresting in volume. For the rest of the winter and into the spring, Nick and I were living in a caretaker's house on a much larger property. The second floor included two bedrooms, one of which opened out to the ocean through large ceiling-to-floor French windows. There was no shower in the bathroom, only a huge Japanese bathtub. The main disadvantage was the lack of hot water. To draw a bath, you had to first heat pots on all four stove burners, then haul the pots upstairs to the tub once the water was hot. "Prince Charles! Prince Charles! Courage!" I'd call out, reminding Nick and myself that ice-cold showers and general suffering were character-building techniques utilised by Queen Elizabeth and Prince Philip on their poor, frozen only son and heir. Nothing could persuade either of us to stay in the tub any longer than to clean each other's backs before vanishing naked and goose-bumpy into a waiting towel.

For the next two weeks, I heated the water on the stove and poured it into the douche bag, along with a dropperful of Turkish mushroom cap tincture and powders distilled from gnome-filled forests, which all smelled uncomfortably like Dr. Mouchotte. The physical writhings that ensued were unfathomable. The cure preparation took up the majority of the day. When I wasn't doubling over in misery and discomfort, I was writing letters to friends and family members about Nick and my new romantic life in our farmhouse in the Alpes-Maritimes.

As a result of my ailments, Nick and my physical relationship had to bridge a few rivers. The trip's charm, I knew, rested on my becoming healthy as soon as possible, but I was already growing tired of the boiling-and-then-cooling of the water. At the same time, the plastic tubing hanging over the toilet inspired my first songs, which I wrote in an attempt to relieve my own anguish and aggravation. Writing songs became an emotional release for me, transforming my own experiences and history into those of another. "I can't stand you" turns into "She can't stand him." "I no longer love you" changed to "She no longer loves him." I was able to free up the words and emotions within me by shifting from me and I to her and she. Just like Monica Vitti or Sophia Loren fleeing away from Nick on the beach.

Six weeks into our stay, Nick and I drove to Spain, stopping along the way in ancient French towns that reminded me of Cézanne and Van Gogh's canvases. We drove via Aix, Les Baux, Arles, Montpellier, Cap d'Agde, Perpignan, and just over the Spanish border, Cadaqués, the village Salvador Dal painted and where Picasso, Miró, and Duchamp stayed. In Cadaqués, Nick and I shared a bright room. It was the first night in weeks that we had hot running water, which we took full advantage of by filling the tub almost to overflowing. Our stay was fantastic, and I attributed my tranquillity to one thing: I didn't quiver. Nick and I made love after a long hiatus, which also helped reduce any symptoms of "the vibrations." We left the next day for Barcelona. I felt my spirit break in half when I first saw what I believed was the city, brash and ugly and charmless, with factories and pollution filling the air, and was relieved to realise that the city I saw was Badalona, on the seacoast 45 minutes northeast of Barcelona. What a difference a letter can make. Nick drove us to

Barcelona at breakneck pace, where we had a reservation at the Avenida Palace. A wonderful city, a total relief.

That night at dinner, I saw a woman at another table who reminded me so much of Chibie that I burst into tears. My grandmother had died of a heart attack the summer before, only a week after I fainted in front of Odetta. I'd been having mild anxiety episodes since then, afraid of losing control in the same manner I'd lost control onstage in front of Odetta. The dam finally burst that night during dinner. I cried for so long and so loudly that the waiters and formally attired diners around us noticed, and the maître d' got so concerned that he arrived at our table with cold clothes. Nick was concerned and was about to call an ambulance. Instead, we made our way out of the dining room, me with my torso bent down and collapsing against Nick's shoulder. We were both perplexed. What was the situation? That night, I stayed awake, shaking, and only fell asleep after a hot bath and a phenobarbital.

I called my mother from my hotel room early the next morning, still in Barcelona, and detailed my symptoms. Mommy had just gotten interested in psychoanalysis and saw a famous practitioner in New York, a Freud disciple named Dr. Albert Lowenstein, on occasion. Mommy contacted me back later that morning after checking with him. Based on my symptoms, she and Dr. Lowenstein suspected I was having a "nervous breakdown," for which Daddy had been hospitalised twice. We devised a strategy: I would leave, return home, and seek assistance.

I was reading Stendhal's The Red and the Black by the twig-strewn pool on one side of our modest house a week before I went. Tiny water drops blew in from the sea and up the Alps' slopes, reflecting the sparkling hues of the alpine flowers. It was the mistral, a powerful, cold, sick wind similar to the sirocco that bulldozes across Africa or the magical Santa Ana winds in Southern California, I discovered. As I read my book, leaves piled up thickly on the bottom of the dirty pool, engrossed by its melodrama, longing, and romance.

Nick drove me to Nice the next morning. On the boat to Europe and throughout my stay, I fantasised about meeting French musicians who would show up at our house carrying guitars, lutes, flutes, and hand drums, all of us jamming late into the night, the entire scene ending up, inexplicably, in the stands of a Spanish bullfight, with Lady Brett Ashley from Hemingway's The Sun Also Rises. Naturally, none of that had occurred—not even remotely. But, in addition to the homecoming gifts I'd packed for my family, I'd be returning to the States with my Phillips tape recorder and at least three songs I'd composed, two with Nick as lyricist. While not as many or as many as I had intended, those three melodies signified a start.

* * *

Dr. Lowenstein had recommended an old-school Freudian analyst, so I started therapy right away. I lay down on Dr. F's couch five days a week, never ever glancing at him, and he remained mute in exchange, giving me plenty of time to think about the Rorschach-like drawings of trees and cucumbers that covered the walls. During my sessions, I experienced brief bouts of anxiety. I'd sit up on the couch, bury my face between my knees, take deep breaths, and try to find answers to the mystery of what was wrong with me. I had numerous nightmares involving Billy and Ronny, but Dr. F and I never figured out what they meant—or I just didn't trust his interpretations. I could periodically hear his pen scribbling, and as I entered and exited his office, I received little glances of a nice-looking man whose unfocused right eye gave him a slightly comical—or perhaps magical—expression.

What was the most significant outcome of my sessions with Dr. F? I hadn't had the shakes since returning to New York. I'd come to assume that my trembling was caused by my relationship with Nick.

Dr. F also spent a lot of time questioning me about Ronny, despite the fact that I was too shy to talk about anything vital or intimate. I'd always known about Mommy and Ronny in some deep part of myself, and their involvement was suddenly public. Mommy and Ronny could be seen everywhere four years after Daddy's death: on the Riverdale library couch, in the garden planting bulbs, kissing in the kitchen, strolling my mother's Dalmatians, Mandy and Pandy. My mother's social circle had to have known. What were their thoughts? I was perplexed. Did they slander each other? Did they give a damn?

I could never comprehend Mommy's unself-conscious ease about her romance with Ronny, and I couldn't accept that any remorse she felt ceased the moment Daddy died. I was still not forgiving Ronny. I despised him. His speaking accent always had a fake quality to it, as if he was listening to his own voice on a tape recorder and wondered how it compared to Ezio Pinza.

Dr. F gently told me at the end of my analysis, which coincided with the expiration of the modest inheritance my father had given me, that it was time to graduate, that together, we had gotten to the source of my psychological problems. He assured me that from now on, I would be significantly better capable of dealing with any circumstance that arose. In retrospect, I believe he must have caught a whiff of the strong, sour aroma of future rejected checks, the scent of a patient on the verge of running out of finances.

* * *

Nick had returned to New York by this point, and we went out to dinner at Chez Napoleon on West Fifty-fifth Street to celebrate my psychoanalytic "graduation." The wine list that night had Châteauneuf-du-Pape, the same wine we had shipped every night in France. Nick and I ate flounder, oysters, and onions in cream sauce while reminiscing about our days and nights in the Alpes-Maritimes over a shared bottle, both of us aware that we had been in that stage of our relationship where couples who love each other say good-bye in slow motion before moving on to others.

We walked all the way to the East Side, where I lived with my sister Joey on Fifty-fifth Street and First Avenue. Nick left me there because it was no longer clear where he was going to spend the night. I fell asleep while watching a movie and was awakened a few hours later by a rumbling throughout my body—the identical shakes that had brought me to psychoanalysis in France. They had returned. Why? Was I having a bad day? Is it possible that seeing Nick reawakened some old recollection of our friendship in France that had returned at the restaurant? Then it dawned on me: it was the red wine, Châteauneuf-du-Pape! When Nick and I were in Europe, we drank this wine virtually every night. It wasn't a nervous breakdown at all, like the ultimate twist in an O. Henry narrative, but rather allergies. If I'd gone to an allergist instead of wasting all that time, not to mention my inheritance, on Dr. F's couch, I might still be in France with Nick, buying small Matisses and Picassos in seaside villages.

Aside from allergies, I had to determine whether or not to return to college. My mother, Joey, and Lucy had all seen me perform on stage. Nick was the only one who pressed me to continue my study, and I loved him all the more for being on the losing side of this discussion, and not least for accompanying me, hand in hand, through the mistral's trials. I honestly didn't know what I wanted. I would have gone in any route that everyone else seemed to be certain of. I saw no reason to return to Sarah Lawrence and was delighted, if not relieved, to put my formal education on hold indefinitely. Lucy and I had rapidly issued a second album by then, and we were singing all over the country, but the problem was that I didn't want to keep doing it. To be honest, I didn't have any huge new musical objectives until I fell in love with Willie Donaldson.

Chapter 8: Record Numero Uno

In 1970, everything felt new to me: my Murray Hill neighbourhood, my physical and emotional proximity to Jake, and the fact that I was living alone for the first time in my life, just me and my fluffy fake-fur foldout couch, my clothes, my shoes, and my music, strewn around five wildly imaginative Stanford White rooms. (It was a look, a style, and a type of architecture that I tried to emulate everywhere I went from then on.) In the space I dubbed "my office," I'd put up my new sound system, which contained all of my newest, highest-fidelity equipment.

Jake invited me over to his place for an Indian takeout meal one night in the winter of 1970. (Dinner at Jake's was basically an open invitation.) Janet Margolin, who starred in the film David and Lisa, was present, as was her husband, Jerry Brandt. Jerry was a music manager who worked with the Harlem Boys Choir and other artists. I wasn't sure if Jake had scripted this introduction for professional reasons, but Jake asked me to play our new song somewhere between the raita and the naan.

Jerry was ecstatic when I completed singing "That's the Way..." "Can you and I get together?" he inquired. "Would you like to make a record?"

Jerry tossed the coins, translating their significance by going to the page referencing the coin pattern. I was an I Ching novice back then, as I am today, and I think the answer was likely to be construed in whatever way the coin toss decided. If I recall correctly, the answer in this case has to do with a bear declining to step on the mouse's foot and instead opting to take on bigger difficulties, such as a moose. It may have been something different, but the fundamental question of whether Jerry and I should collaborate was answered in the affirmative.

Jerry asked if I knew the guitarist David Bromberg, which I did. Jerry offered to assemble a group of musicians to help construct a tape that he could take around to several record companies and try to sell me to one of them as a solo artist, possibly sparking a bidding war.

We were in action all of a sudden. The next thing I knew, I was in an uptown studio with Dave Bromberg and several other musicians, recording three of my songs—"That's the Way I've Always Heard It Should Be," "Alone," and "I'm All It Takes to Make You Happy"— as well as two songs by unknown writers. Jerry watched the entire time and, like me, departed the studio with a tape. Still, there remained an underlying concern in the back of my mind: why was I recording two songs by other songwriters when I knew I just wanted to utilise my songs as demos for myself as a composer?

As far as I was aware, I was simply consenting to record some demos, which would then be distributed to other musicians, who could exclaim, "Wow!—what a wonderful song—and perfect for me." They'd record it, and I'd be off to the bank, perhaps accompanied by some kind of minor celebrity: my name on a piece of sheet music, that sort of thing. Whatever state of denial I was in, I still hold some semblance of it today. I can't seem to totally commit to becoming a performer. Even when I'm performing, I keep trying to get off the stage sooner rather than later.

* * *

Elektra Records allegedly hosted weekly lunch meetings when everyone at the label gathered around a large round table to listen to that week's submissions. The voting process was democratic. When my recording was played, every single person in the room voted it down, according to a photographer on staff. No one appeared to know who I was stylistically or how to sell me. Was I a jazz vocalist? A pop star? What is a folkie? Elektra's president, Jac

Holzman, had the authority to veto whatever he felt passionately about, and he used it this time. "There's something about her that I just feel," he added, news that Jerry Brandt recounted to me the next day. Elektra Records was interested in me! I was all in! I was all in!

Jac and I immediately started talking about producers. Jac noted that he had recently finished working on the Joe Cocker album Mad Dogs and Englishmen with Eddie Kramer. He arranged for a meeting with Eddie, who arrived at my place and listened to me play piano and sing "That's the Way...," "Alone," and a few other songs before I picked up my guitar and played a few of my guitar-based compositions. Eddie was from South Africa. Even if he didn't have Willie's posh accent, I was a hopeless Anglophile (and that obviously included South Africa and most certainly Australia!) who could have gladly feast on accents ranging from Cockney to Cantabrigian, with anything in between. They brought back Willie's greatest memories. It was just a matter of time until Eddie and I found ourselves in the East Coast's Electric Lady Studios on Eighth Street in Greenwich Village.

Among the many people I saw wandering the halls of Electric Lady was Jimi Hendrix, his nostrils smudged, followed by throngs of half-naked, elaborately painted girls, their own nostrils quite white, the whole crew on their way to a back restroom that I later discovered was elaborately painted in psychedelic colours.

"That's the Way..." was the very first song Eddie and I recorded. Of course, that made sense, and it was also the tune with which I was most familiar. Eddie recorded it with just me on piano and a metronome to keep time. Then I met Ed Freeman, a fantastic arranger who not only arranged the string parts wherever they were needed, but also assisted me with what are known as "head arrangements"—that is, just enough information for the musicians to follow in order to communicate that "non-arrangement" feel, but enough organisation or structure to keep everyone on the same page.

Then things became a little more complex.

To be honest, I was uneasy being alone in the studio with the engineer, Dave Palmer. Dave was excellent at what he did, but I made up for it by being a complete amateur. Not only did I not know what to do, but I feigned to know what to do and ended up mixing almost half the album (a listener can easily identify which tracks I had a hand in mixing today). In retrospect, Dave must have felt confused about this tall, unknown girl with an overbite taking over at the board and urging him to "lower the reverb and add compression, also bring up the snare, my vocal is too soft on the second chorus."

Another painful moment was when Jerry Brandt informed me that he would no longer be my manager. Janet, his wife, didn't want him getting too close to me, nor did she want Jerry and me spending so much time together. All I could imagine was that Jerry had lost faith in my abilities or that, knowing Eddie Kramer was no longer engaged in the production, he felt my first album would be a flop. I was so unhappy that I'm surprised I finished the record at all, but thanks to Steve Harris, Jac, and his brother Keith, who stepped in to spend a lot of time in the studio, I did.

Finally, Jac, Keith, and Steve persuaded Eddie and me to reconcile our disagreements, and urged Eddie to return to Electric Lady to complete recording the few tracks that hadn't yet been finished, and especially to mix "That's the Way I've Always Heard It Should Be." Of all the songs, that was the one Jac felt most confident in and eager to hear in its final form. It's no surprise that Jac was so influential on the artists he mentored. He was an elegantly ferocious gentleman with a strong sense of self, whereas Steve Harris was pleasant, witty, and cheerful. The outcome was my debut record, simply titled Carly Simon.

But how should I handle the cover art? I'd posed uncomfortably on a studio floor a few weeks before for a full-body, leaning-on-my-shoulder, head-to-one-side shot. The creative director eventually chose to crop the photo to create a frontal head shot, rotating it 45 degrees to the right to make it appear as if I was looking directly at the camera. Even yet, one side of my face couldn't help but look as if gravity was tugging it to the floor. My makeup left a large bruise on one cheek, which retouching never fixed. My brother Peter photographed me again at his farm in Massachusetts, this time in a long pink frock with my legs crossed below me. The other photo, which came up on the back cover, would eventually have an interesting consequence. I looked a lot like Mick Jagger in it. It's possible that Mick and I did look similar, but that photo made people—including Mick himself—aware of the similarities.

I was damned if I thought beyond the artwork and credits once the record was finished. I needed a break or, even crazier, a vacation. I had no desire to promote my album with a tour or television appearances. Why? Stage fright, plain and simple, or, more specifically, my dread of stage fright. I had no desire to confront my many phobias. I merely wanted my album to serve as a demo and showcase for my songs, so that other singers could wish to record them later.

My dread of performing onstage, combined with a slew of other nagging phobias that were impeding my progress, drove me into the arms of one of the smartest, most empathetic, and entertaining psychiatrists I'd ever met. I'll refer to him as Dr. L. He was also motivated to assist me in overcoming the challenges on my path. Anxiety over performance. High-strung-ness. Problems with self-esteem. My sessions with Dr. L would last years.

In the weeks following the completion of my album, another album was on my turntable at all hours of the day and night, an album I memorised and sang along with, and I'm sure millions of other women throughout the country were doing the same: James Taylor's Sweet Baby James. Joey and I were going home from the movies on

Fifty-ninth Street one night when we noticed a newsstand selling the new issue of Time magazine, which had a cartoon drawing of James Taylor's face on the front with the title THE NEW ROCK: BITTERSWEET AND LOW. I confidently blurted out, "I'm going to marry him." How did I find out? Over the years, people have questioned me. The only explanation I can think of is that he, James, was perfect for me in every aspect. If you believe in predestination or clairvoyance, this is an excellent example of why you are correct.

* * *

My album was released in February 1971 to mostly positive reviews. In March of that year, while standing in the tiny kitchen of my Murray Hill apartment, I received a crucial phone call. Elektra's Jac Holzman and Steve Harris were on the other end of the line. "What would it take for you to open for Cat Stevens at the Troubadour on April 6?" they wanted to know.

I became immobile. The deadline was in less than three weeks. I had no desire or intention of performing live by myself—I had sung many times before, but never on a stage for critics, never without Lucy, never with a real band or for a promotion. I lived in New York, the Troubadour was in Los Angeles, and my growing phobia of flying was exacerbated by the fact that I'd be flying to do anything. I wanted to hang up, but I was also thinking quickly. James Taylor was touring with a band that included drummer Russ Kunkel. I knew Russ Kunkel was the best drummer to come around in a long time. All that was required was to pick up the needle and listen to the tom-tom fills on "Fire and Rain" and "Country Road." I cleverly informed Jac and Steve that if they could get Russ Kunkel to be my drummer, I would agree to do it, knowing full well that getting Russ was impossible. Jac and Steve had no idea how quick-witted I could be when confronted with my own anxieties, nor could they (or I) have anticipated how fate can occasionally throw you for a loop.

I didn't have a manager at the time, so I had to rely on Steve Harris, Elektra's A&R man, to stay close by and schedule all of our cross-country plane travels and hotel reservations. It was my first visit to California, and I was frightened of flying. Nonetheless, Steve and I travelled first class out west, me floating on ten milligrams of Valium and Steve levitating above me on four times that much. It was the golden age of air travel, with stylish but probably bacteria-infested upper decks, bars, and even piano players. Steve spent the majority of the flight telling me Jim Morrison war stories. Three or four hours into the ride, Steve pointed out the Grand Canyon and the Rockies, both of which I, a mostly sheltered East Coast girl, had never seen before.

I ran into Kris Kristofferson, who was with T Bone Burnett and Stephen Bruton, the guitarist and songwriter, as I was heading through the Hyatt lobby to check in. Kris introduced himself, and we had a brief chat, the type of which Kris excelled, one in which meaning and connotation are crammed into the shortest, punchiest interchange. Kris cracked a few Texan jokes while straining his sunken, intense, icy blue eyes—eyes like a Samoyed, I thought. He had the expression of a man who had just undressed you and knew you wouldn't need any more clothing for a long time. Every sign Kris gave me indicated, "I've got to have you," and I felt possessed.

On opening night, I ditched my customary late-sixties-chic ensemble of lace, beads, and braids in favour of a new, carefully selected ensemble: a dark brown, short-sleeved, mid length dress and high Chelsea Cobbler red leather boots, a present from Jac Holzman when I signed my contract at Elektra. It would just be me, ever vigilant, ever neurotic, and most of all, ever concerned about any terrifying onstage scenario. I was afraid I'd pass out and my band wouldn't be able to revive me. I was afraid I'd vomit. I was concerned that if I vomited, I wouldn't be able to persuade the other members of the band to blame it on a front-row audience member.

Steve Harris grabbed my elbow and held me up as I walked down to the stage with my instruments. The club was small, and each table had a bud vase with a single pink rose. Jimmy, Paul, and Russ were already onstage, which provided some solace, but my entire fear made my hands feel like flippers, clammy and bulbous. What I had to do was take up my guitar, strap it on my head, and start playing. Simple. At the moment. My heart was racing so fast that I wondered if they would bring a phone to me onstage so I could call Dr. L and other specialists.

I stood motionless in front of the audience until I heard a pleasant, familiar voice call out to me. I got sight of Kate Taylor's incredibly lovely, dazzling face as I shielded my eyes from the glare of the lights. Her voice was familiar and reassuring, and when I heard her greeting, my frozen right arm relaxed and fell fortuitously on the first G chord of my first song, "One More Time." The audience erupted in applause. I have no recollection of what I said in between songs, but I had a strong connection with the crowd, and by the fifth and last song, "That's the Way I've Always Heard It Should Be," I strolled confidently over to the piano. If anything, the piano made me more apprehensive than the guitar, but as I started singing, the audience became silent and focused. My father sits in the dark at night... I hear her say "sweet dreams," but I have forgotten how to dream...

During the song, the microphone began to slowly wander to the left. I grabbed it and pulled it back to the middle, but as soon as I let go, it started drifting again. I brought it back to the middle, like a typist on an old-fashioned machine. The sole benefit of my ever-tilting movable mic was that it diverted my attention away from my own anxiety. The crowd, who had observed the quiet, ongoing struggle, was on my side by the end of the song and gave me a standing ovation.

* * *

Backstage, it seemed like the whole Elektra Records staff was crammed into my tiny, flower-filled dressing room, informing me that "That's the Way I've Always Heard It Should Be" had jumped to number 24 on the Cashbox charts. Cat Stevens came over to congratulate me before disappearing into his own dressing area to get his band and guitar. Steve Harris emptied my dressing room of everyone but one man—or was it a large boy?—sprawled on the floor in the far corner of the room once the embraces and congrats had peaked.

James Taylor was the one. I hadn't noticed him before for some reason, but suddenly I knew him right away. He was nodding off slightly, but since I hadn't heard that drug expression yet, all I could think of was James being fatigued. He was barefoot, long-legged, and long-footed, with his knees bent. He was dressed in dark red corduroys with a wide waist and a long-sleeved Henley with one button open, his right hand gripping a self-rolled cigarette. His hair was both shining and tousled, falling evenly on both sides of his head, and he had a scruffy, subtle moustache, the type that was popular in the early 1970s. He appeared to be both kempt and untidy. Everything about him, even when he was spread out on the floor, signalled that he was, in fact, the centre of something—the core of an apple, the centre of a message. James came, and we had a two-minute conversation about the Vineyard. He sat in the corner till the door opened (too soon for me) and Joni Mitchell, James's girlfriend at the time, emerged and said, "James, we have to go now." James got to his feet slowly, nodded to me without making eye contact, and followed her out the door. I wouldn't see him again for seven months, but I kept thinking about him. In person, he and I didn't hit it off right away—James was too stoned—but over the next few days, I reflected on the insane prediction I made the night I saw his face on the cover of Time magazine: that the two of us would someday marry. But how many other ladies had the same fantasy? I'd dissolve into the millions, stupid.

Chapter 9: Carnegie Hall

I was back in New York for Thanksgiving 1971, after a whirlwind of last-minute planning. My diary for the first half of that year was misplaced in a checked suitcase on an American Airlines flight to Palm Springs for an Elektra convention. The loss of my handcrafted Indian outfit with sewn-in beads came in second place to the loss of my diary. My seductive yet politically wrong stage dress (since the American Indians were being ripped off by Madison Avenue) consisted of that and a pair of chamois boots. Sure enough, so much was happening in such a short period of time that my calendars, which were fortunately in my pocketbook on the plane, depict a whirlwind of names, places, and life-changing events.

That Thanksgiving, my single "Anticipation" was already at the top of the charts, and the album of the same name was about to be released. I had just returned from Los Angeles, where I had performed as the closing act at the Troubadour. I was hanging out with drummer Rick Marotta. Our fundamental relationship was founded on music, companionship, and the bond of friendship, and it has lasted for decades. I was drawn to him since his music and sense of humour were both appealing to me.

On the night following Thanksgiving, at 7:30 p.m., I received a call from someone in James Taylor's camp offering me two tickets to his show at Carnegie Hall. ("Jesus-Mary-and-Joseph," as Allie, Chibie, and my mother would say when something unexpected happened.) I didn't have time to contemplate and had to move quickly. Ricky was game, and he was hilarious in the limousine that was magically plucked from a garage in Queens to pick us up for the occasion. The lumbering twelve-seater was silent as it whisked Ricky and me north, transporting me back to a more innocent moment in my New York mind, back to childhood and those car excursions into the city's glistening twilight glow. Ricky and I had been smoking and writing songs all day and were still dressed the same. I was dressed for the folk-rock concert of my dreams, wearing a white Nehru shirt made of a cotton/nylon blend, jeans, and my red Jac Holzman boots. Rick's attractive features were dominated by his beard and long black horsetails that reached halfway down his back. As we stepped out of the automobile, Carnegie Hall appeared spectacular, as if it were thankfully coming from the past.

We walked in but couldn't find our seats. We were late, and our tickets had not been reserved for us at the ticket window, so we sat in the back until intermission. The first half of the event sounded just like the records I was already hooked on. Danny Kortchmar (or "Kooch"), Carole King, Lee Sklar, and Russ Kunkel, who had played with me in L.A. following James' motorbike accident, were in the same band—and the most absolutely appropriate ensemble ever. Carnegie Hall had the best acoustics in the country at the time. James' voice was excellent, clear, and welcoming. His band was completely at ease with all of the songs, which they had performed numerous times and included on Sweet Baby James and Mud Slide Slim and the Blue Horizon, the new album that had catapulted James to international stardom. I could see the painting on the back cover of Mud Slide Slim written all over it as I watched him sing the title tune. Laurie Miller painted it, and it depicted the "cabin in the woods" that James had described, the one built (as the song goes) by "Jimmy, Jimmy, John, Luke, and Laurie, No Jets Construction." (I had no idea I'd meet all of them and see that shack come to life only a week later.) He sang all the songs I knew by heart from his first two albums, as well as "You've Got a Friend," the single that had reached number one on the charts that summer. The fact that I was so close to him was amazing. I had the energy of a zigzagging youngster in my limbs, and I was smiling so wide that my cheeks must have grown permanently larger that night.

Awkwardly, I asked Ricky if it was okay if I went backstage with

Nat. Simply implying. "You bitch," he said quickly, and went back to talking to some pals he'd ran into. It was amusing. Our friendship has lasted considerably longer than any other relationship I had that night. Nat and I headed upstairs to the band's dressing area, where there was food on a big table and a trash can of ice with every kind of cola, spritzer, and Sprite-like drink you could think of. It served as the room's centre fire pit. Everyone looked to be having fun with the sparks, as if there were marshmallows to be roasted.

***

In the two hours between James falling into his sweet place of slumber and waking up, I don't think I experienced anything more than a minor dimming of my consciousness. I was lying awake, his songs playing in my thoughts, till there was a mixing of sounds, both silent, feminine and male, and I coaxed my melodies to melt into his. My lips moved in silence. "His pastures to change … deep greens and blues are the colours I choose … down in my dreams…"

I was singing to him in my head, the part that was thoughtfully unthinking. Singing as well as singing. "Blossom, send some sunshine my way... I've been feeling lonely lately." The tunes alternated, and I stayed restless and extremely inspired. "There's a well on the hill, you just can't kill for Jesus, there's a well on the hill, let it be." And after that, I sang my own lyrics about him: "Then you turn on the radio and sing with the singer in the band, and think kind of sadly to yourself, this isn't exactly what you had planned … "Because you're a legend in your own time, a hero in the footlights, playin' tunes to fit your rhyme, but a legend's only a lonely boy when he goes home alone."

My muse, my Orpheus, my sleeping darling, my "good night, sweet prince," my something-in-the-way-he-moves was James. The bedroom was dark and quiet, with only a few slats of light filtering in through the louvred shutters. I gently moved my right hand's fingers down his left arm to his shoulder, over his slopes, so as not to wake him.

When we moved from the living room to the bedroom the night before, he replied, "Let's just go to sleep." I wholeheartedly agreed. Let's put off what we're both terrified of, I reasoned. He went on to say that we had both been playing the field, and that this shouldn't have happened. We knew it wouldn't be a one-night stand. There were numerous things we already knew. Many years later, he'd accuse me of liking him for "being James Taylor," which he meant in a derogatory way. But it was spot on and a perfect representation of how I felt.

* * *

It was just getting light outside, and I could see the closet door with the mirror, which caught a part of our bodies in a grey charcoal mist, from my bedroom.

Everything else was hazy, and the single candle that had burned all night was still the brightest thing in the room. We were still in a lovely knot. I hadn't moved except to relieve numbness in one of my legs by slipping my ankle from beneath his calf very slowly. He hadn't stirred at the time, but when he did, he awoke lustful. He immediately kissed me. The gesture was so natural and straightforward. I let his lips around mine. Two pairs of lips may find each other with two sets of eyes closed.

He was at ease, and our bodies did the Bali Ha'i dance, with only the sound of waves breaking and blankets moving and cushions muffled the high-end frequency of the sheets brushing together. The quantity of energy that had accumulated over the two hours (mine as I remained still and his while he slept) gave way to openness unfettered by self-consciousness. James kissed me on the cheek, and I returned his affection. The sounds that notes generate when they are played together have varied properties. That's all we were, two notes.

We were a fantastic fourth, in my opinion. I began to feel like the F-sharp and he was the C-sharp. A lot of singing together over the years appeared to confirm this. Our voices were so wonderfully complementary and matched. His voice, with its clear and delicate tone, slipped in like an oboe cutting through the breathy rising of an alto flute. This music theory, like the love theory, has yet to be proved or demonstrated. Like some things, it might be true only if I continue to believe it.

Chapter 10: Choppin' Wood

My family would always rent or borrow properties on the island when I was a kid, whether in Chilmark, Menemsha, or West Tisbury. The Taylors, who arrived on the island in 1953, were up-islanders who lived in a house in Chilmark. Unlike Mommy and Daddy, who always rented, the Taylors were full-time islanders, at first only for the summers until Trudy, James's mother, made the gorgeous, rustic house on Stonewall Beach in Chilmark her permanent home.

With our Martha's Vineyard connection, James and I spoke about the island in a kind of code, as if we shared a hidden language we'd both grown up speaking—which we did. We started making preparations to go almost as soon as we met, excited to explore places we both knew so well and had seen without the other for decades. James' spirit was on the Vineyard, on his land, and mine would eventually settle there as well. James, like his father, had found and purchased his own large piece of land in 1969, but on the opposite end of the island, in the Lambert's Cove region of Tisbury—175 acres of woods, primarily scrub oak, tangles of lady's slippers, wild berries, cedar, cypress, and pine. James had also gotten a terrific bargain, purchasing the land with money from Apple Records for his first record. Aside from being wild and rolling, it was secluded and close enough to his parents' house for simple gatherings. He lived with a huge pig named Mona and his puppy, David, who was part wolf and quarter German shepherd. James' goal was to build a homestead atop the hill, which he was excited to show me.

James moved into my Murray Hill apartment immediately after that first night, the flawless meshing of the gears of our lives already perfectly in place, as if they had been there forever. There was no sense of urgency or pressure. Later that morning, the two of us retrieved all of his belongings from the Barbizon-Plaza, placing messages into a small suitcase labelled JT. He packed yet another bag full of dog-chewed footwear. James' motel room was as disorganised as a teen's. James left a twenty-dollar payment for the housekeepers, but everything else we carried back to Murray Hill—and he and I were never apart for more than a few days for the rest of the time.

We walked up to Manny's Music on 48th Street the day after our first night together. Our arrival into the store became a sort of watershed moment, formally establishing us as a pair, the musical equivalent of a billboard advertisement. Manny's owner, Henry Goldrich, made a big deal out of it, even asking if he could place our photos together on the store's Wall of Fame. Of course, we both said that we would be honoured. Our portraits were already in the house, but they were far apart, so Henry positioned mine next to James's, prominently, at eye level.

* * *

We drove to the Vineyard in James' green pickup less than two weeks later to view his "cabin in the woods"—the "shack," as James kept referring to it. Having spent my Vineyard summers up-island, I had always hoped to one day own a home there, perhaps in Chilmark, directly on the sea. In contrast, James' enormous estate seemed out of place, as if it belonged on the south shore. The area was closer to the down-island sections of the Vineyard I was less familiar with, near the water but without beach access. It was as if James was underlining the necessity and worth of maintaining a more modest workaday image—announcing to the world that he wasn't the son of an acclaimed physician who'd gone to Harvard, but rather a man who worked with his hands and had the calluses to prove it. We had no idea the land would become a life-long project for both of us.

I recall our arrival and our first night there. We drove off Lambert's Cove Road into James' driveway, driving the quarter-mile distance

79

slowly, while the moon came up in the east, to our left, seemingly following us as we made our way along the long dirt road. James later told me that he was afraid about what I would think, that I would be one of those stiff New York-at-heart girls who was strongly opinionated about the peasant order. I could see the outlines of what appeared to be a lovely music box of a house ahead of us. James' cabin was silhouetted in the moonlight. The roof had a severe pitch. The windows were both tall and narrow. Everything in the house was tall, lean, modest, and gorgeous, much like James.

We took a lengthy stroll around the property the next morning (I borrowed Kate's walking shoes). James escorted me through low forests of packed new-growth pine and scrub oak, fall clematis, and blueberry plants that had been virtually crushed to the ground by the first frost, all of which belonged to James. The property exuded maturity. What did it actually mean to be a landowner? I'm sure my parents—and other adults—knew those rules and answers, but I didn't, at least not at the time. The area had deep crevasses, rolling hills, and steep ridges, as if the entire acreage had been carved by some kind of massive glacial action aeons ago. It was and still is the most hilly region of the island. The soil was normally sandy but heavy and fertile enough to sustain towering trees and fat crops over time, and while James' acreage wasn't on the water, it was close enough for the air to smell of salt and sea.

I had no doubts about him. Already, he was having rock walls built by a local artisan, one of the numerous builders who were assisting James in realising his vision. There was a young hippy group who lived on James' acreage, created things with their hands, and hung out at James' cabin, offering their ideas, aptitudes, and abilities. I couldn't have predicted the profound hold James's cabin would have on me at the time. I remember being cautious to make any recommendations during my first few trips, not wanting to seem intrusive, especially because James's vision for the place was still unfolding, and he'd done everything from sawing and nailing wood to hand-sewing the shower curtain. Should I suggest that he place a door on the bathroom? Or was that too conventional a concept, the kind of excessively civilised suggestion that went against the fundamental idea of living a straightforward Vineyard life? Maybe it was just that I didn't want to admit how hard I was pre-nesting. (Warning: there will be comfort!) James and I didn't discuss any of this right away, especially where the two of us would live if we stayed together. But one night, full of love, James had a foresight. He assured me that if our relationship survived and we were married, we would have two children. First, there would be a little girl named Sarah, and then, a few years later, a boy named Ben, according to him.

James walked into the woods to the woodpile after leaving the cabin. It was a cold night with a nearly full moon, I recall. I soon heard the noises of beating on the ground. James must have felt relieved and proud of himself for defying Kate's wretched Green Beret. Perhaps he was punishing himself as well, picking up an axe and unleashing whatever brutality he imagined on Hank against a pile of helpless logs. I couldn't help but think of the lines from Philip Larkin's collection of poems Willie had given me: "This is the first thing / I have understood: / Time is the echo of an axe / Within a wood." Then, all of a sudden, the chopping halted, and James cried into the starry night, "CARLY, I LOVE YOU!"

When he got home, he put some freshly split wood in the Franklin stove and lit it up (James always "lit it up," striking a match against the underside of the kitchen counter or against the sole of his shoe). After starting the fire, he shut the glass doors on the stove and turned out to save one small bulb near our pullout bed. He returned upstairs before retiring to see how Kate was doing. That night, in my opinion, James had grasped the moment, safeguarded his sister, had a catharsis, and sang my name up to the moon in a fit of love-crazed wood cutting. And I was letting that love in, reflecting it back to him. Being with James felt more like a magical fate to me than a choice.

James reappeared downstairs and disappeared into the doorless bathroom, where he cleaned the soot and ash from his hands. He approached our bed in no rush, still dressed and wearing his boots. His boots (I believe they were made by White's) raised him two inches above his already tall, toned six-foot-two-and-a-half-inch frame. He was dressed in a light brown and blue plaid work shirt. His turquoise belt buckle was loosened, and his jeans dropped down unevenly over his boots, saggy at the knees and undone at the waist. I could see his eyes in the lamplight: they were a brilliant blue. I'd never seen that colour blue light up the dark in such a way, those two eyes gazing at me wide open, a breathing, cursing, loving, wanting blueness that moved me beyond all words.

As James approached, the space between us shrank, and our perpendicular lines, like the surge of a waterfall, became parallel. Our existence together would continue in this manner for quite some time.

* * *

From the beginning, James and I were inextricably tied not only by love and music, but also because we were both damaged people trying to pass as normal. It was difficult for both of us to act as if we were at peace in the world. It was a relief to have a reprieve from our private, unique craziness in each other. Before we met, James had been famously written about. He'd dropped out of Milton Academy, a prep school outside of Boston, in his junior year and gone to McLean Hospital, which also provided instruction. Many of his first album's tracks, like "Night Owl" and "Knocking 'Round the Zoo," were inspired by the people or situations he encountered there. Whatever his diagnosis was, it was most likely complex, a result of his magnificent, tough brain, which led to sadness and drug addiction. Both were and still are inextricably linked.

If I was in difficulty, James would always come to my aid, even though I knew he felt he didn't belong on this planet as much as I did. I'm not sure if he truly understood my emotions of isolation and being on the outside practically all of the time. Unless I was with him. I preferred to focus on James regardless of the situation, and I would always strive to be helpful. (Of course, this occasionally resulted in me trying too hard and being pushy, obnoxious, cloying, or overdoing it in general.) If James was in pain, his anguish took my focus away from myself, and as a result, I anguished less about myself. It's like having a parent: even if you have the worst migraine on the planet, when your child is sick, your self-centred immersion dissolves into irrelevance, giving way instead to the purity and relief of unselfish caretaking. Diane Johnson portrays a character holding her children's hands as they cross the street in her novel The Shadow Knows. The mom wonders how her children may possibly trust her when she cannot trust herself. The same could be said for James and me. For the following decade, he and I would clutch each other's hands against the onslaught of the curious, the jealous, and the knife-wielding smilers.

For the first few months, James and I commuted from New York to the Vineyard, where we sprayed some new paint, hammered a few nails, and cleared some fields, all while planting some new, real trees (anything not the enormous oak or pine). There was always the splendour of the outdoors on Lambert's Cove, wood to cut, sassafras to plum for tea, and a cellar to clean. I was learning that owning a home was very different from renting. For example, I had no idea if our apartment building on 35th Street had a basement.

We didn't want to socialise in New York other than coparenting James's huge puppy, David. We cooked, drank, and ate. James had a few recipes that he would ultimately become well renowned for: beans, for example, an entirely exceptional Jamesian recipe that included a lot of garlic and onions and steeped for days. James slept late most days and went out with Arlyne or socialised with Jake, Carinthia, Ellen, David, and Mary Ellen at night. We were both uncomfortable with friends or idle time. We were so used to being "on" while we were out in public that being alone in our apartment felt nearly foreign—and almost always: a big relief. We became anxious and restless, always juggling ideas about what to do and when to do it, rapidly feeling irritated with ourselves if we stayed at home when so many people expected us to attend their parties, shows, or get-togethers.

When I flew to Los Angeles to record a demo, James stayed behind in New York to help record a few cuts for Abigale Haness, the girl backstage at the Carnegie Hall concert who would later marry Danny Kortchmar. My phone rang early one morning. It was 3 a.m. in Los Angeles and 6 a.m. on the East Coast. It was James, and his story had nothing to do with Abigail's recording session, but rather with the unusual plumbing in our Stanford White apartment complex. That morning, James was taking a shower when the hot water ran out. When he found himself unexpectedly under a torrent of chilly water, he turned off the cold faucet but forgot to turn off the hot. He went about his job, spending the rest of the day in Nyack, an hour north of New York, recording Abigale. Our building's hot water turned back on somewhere during the day, including, of course, the water in the shower stall. He returned to our apartment, which resembled a Ukrainian steam room sans the old naked men. The wallpaper in the main room was curling off in shreds. The photos and posters were curling inward, and my record collection was warping. All of our photos were destroyed, though some I was able to sort out between the pages of hefty volumes. We eventually had to leave for three months while the entire property was re-wallpapered.

The instant I found out what had transpired was less crucial than the wallpaper. "Is this Carly?" asked the soothing voice on the other end.

"This is James Taylor." James Taylor, not James. As if, after four months of the best propinquity, he was afraid I'd mix him with another James. In times of stress, James's fine manners, courtesy, and old-fashioned North Carolina gentlemanliness shone through. I honestly couldn't care less about the hot water, the wallpaper, or the quality of our record albums, all of which seemed ridiculous and replaceable: all I cared about was that the sweetest, kindest, least replaceable man on the planet was on the other end of the phone.

"My Darling James," I wrote in my diary around that time, "you are so uncommon in my life." What a unique experience. I hope nothing ever changes your status. In so many respects, I've never felt so connected to anyone. That's the key—the mix of proximity. I've had sisters and friends I could share intimate thoughts with, and men I could love but not talk to—uncles and aunts I could easily live with, and men I could talk to but not love—I've had a dog I could snuggle up to and bathtubs that could surround me with warmth, and a grandmother who impressed eccentricity in its most precious forms on me—but you, my Darling, leave me in a new space. You're all in it, and then some."

It was correct. James was the ultimate Orpheus of all my fantasies from the moment I saw a photo of him. He was astute. He was amusing. He was a long, slim, poetical stalk of a guy, and he was stunning to look at. He was anyone's romantic dream of a poet and musician, and listening to him made me feel as if he'd never had to be taught anything, as if he'd been born knowing everything. There's no doubt that the amount of attention James was receiving at the time intimidated me as well. In the early 1970s, James Taylor was the most talked-about singer and composer in music, and everyone wanted him, though I never thought that would impress me. I also believed that if James fell in love with me, I would never doubt myself or my own attractiveness again. (Sure, sure. And no. But I'll get to that later.) James also reminded me of my own father, with his combination of musicianship, worldliness, and dryness, as well as his physical height, blended with an unfathomable darkness and grief, attributes that hinted at something more than what was obvious. My father had been present yet absent, and James had a similar attitude: I'm simply passing through—this apartment, this city, this planet. Daddy had practically never looked me in the eyes for more than a split second, and James, too, had a habit of breaking his focus, usually to stare down at his own feet.

Several years later, when Jake became a Sufi devotee and student, I learned about a highly intimate practice called trespasso, which I convinced James to undertake with me. I stared into one of James's eyes for ten minutes, following which we were supposed to switch roles, with James's two eyes staring attentively into one of mine. We were meant to do the same with the second eye after ten minutes. James, I recall, despised it. He could only gaze at me with rage, as if I were infringing on his mind and soul, probably because I'd forced him to perform this bizarre thing with me in the first place. I wasn't quite at ease with trespasso—it made me self-conscious, and I was strongly aware of James's discomfort. I remember being surprised by how enraged James grew in the first two or three minutes our eyes met. I could feel the waves of aggression flowing off him despite his shuttered expression.

When James and I became a famous couple—perhaps more in print and in our fans' imaginations than in our bedroom and living room—I discovered that the same fire that ignited our relationship could turn to icy silence, to "no-ness," to "can't-go-there-ness," to "we don't talk about that-ness." I accepted this dualism along with the rest of James Taylor's package, most likely because I was accustomed to the same trait in my own father. Furthermore, as Mark Twain famously stated, "everyone is a moon, and has a dark side which he never shows to anybody." "Angry dawns" strikes again! So, while James was my enchanted Orpheus, he was also Heathcliff, flirting with both hot and icy shadows and devils.

There was also the fact that we were both performers who were frequently in the headlines. My career and the attention I was receiving had happened quickly. Cat Stevens performed first, followed by Kris Kristofferson, Don McLean, and Harry Chapin. After James and I met, I went on a multi-city tour with him, doing roughly 10 shows in total. In March 1972, a few months into our relationship, James and I travelled to Hawaii, and on the way back, we stopped in San Francisco to pick up a rental car so we could drive down the California coast to Los Angeles. That night in New York, the Grammy Awards were held, and both of us were nominated, myself for Best New Artist of the Year and James for Best Pop Vocal Performance, Male. We weren't planning on being there in person. I can't say how James felt about the possibility of receiving, or not receiving, a Grammy—he remained silent on the subject—but I was discreetly focused on it, though I made it a point not to say anything to him.

By two a.m., fog was coming in from the Pacific, and that, combined with our jet lag and restlessness, drove our choice to stop along the way and nap, despite the fact that we didn't have any reservations anywhere. We arrived at the Big Sur Lodge despite barely being able to see the highway ahead of us. Fortunately, management had space, and the two of us made our way through the mist to a modest cabin among the redwoods. We discovered a telegram addressed to James Taylor and Carly Simon taped on the door. It was opened by one of us. It was from Elektra's Jac Holzman, and it said, "Congratulations! You both earned Grammys! Jac, love." The most astonishing aspect was that darling Jac had sent a telegraph to every single inn and motel along the route, knowing simply that James and I were travelling down the coast from San Francisco to L.A.

Chapter 11: We'll Marry

We spent the weekend before I left for London on the Vineyard. James and I went so far as to sign an informal prenuptial agreement on a piece of paper on the plane there, anticipating our impending separation. He wrote his remarks on both sides of a single lined paper with a ballpoint pen, and we both knelt to sign it. "This document will attest that James Vernon Taylor and Carly Elizabeth Simon will enter into a state of wedlock as defined therein..." at the time. James' calligraphy was childish, lovely, alternately clean and ardent, wilder. All tangible goods would be deemed common property, and upon "the dissolution of this agreement," all possessions would be returned to their original owner. Joint property will be divided equally "to both parties." In terms of "divorce" (sp), James stated that it would be "applied for in writing, listing grievances," with a "waiting period of three months before compliance." We wrote our names under the pledge, "I hereby agree to the above stipulations," James' signature forky, all bent wire, like a Calder mobile; mine girlish, well-behaved, prep-school-like, lined up beneath his. I still have this lovely, heartbreaking document.

Looking back, we must have taken the choice to marry only four days before the wedding on purpose, giving us no time to worry about the arrangements. Nat Weiss, James's lawyer, arranged for the licence, the limousine, and the Wasserman test 24 hours before the wedding, and James and I made a quick drive down to City Hall in New York for a stamp here, a stamp there. Danny and Abigail Kortchmar would testify for us. Yes, it was a big decision, but it felt right in every sense, especially when you only have a few days to pull your hair out fretting about it. We celebrated with a drink and chicken wings at a Chinese restaurant after signing our names on the City Hall ledger.

With only four days until our wedding, we had to maintain the different processes and ceremonies in order. After the signing, James and I took a lengthy walk through the Village, as unassuming as any two persons could be. On Eighth Street, it was warm and almost dark, and anyone watching us would have assumed we were just another couple out for a stroll, which we were. We went by a jewellery store on MacDougal Street, a few doors off Bleecker Street, promoting wedding bands at a discount—25 PERCENT OFF! shouted the sign on the window.

James and I walked right into the full-price ring section. We knew not to buy rings on sale because they were shady or questionable, but because of some mutually agreed-upon superstition that they were bad luck. Behind the counter appeared a dark, attractive woman. James cast a quick, close, and familiar glance at her before returning his attention to his own shoes. The saleswoman was tall, with an aristocratic posture, her hair in a tight bun, and a white button-down shirt tucked into a black skirt. Her sexy-frosty appearance stood in stark contrast to the tinny, exotic music playing overhead and the flashy chains, Indian fabrics, scarves, crystal rings, various-sized Buddhas, incense sticks, and handcrafted Christmas tree ornaments strung around the shop, winking, shining, and zigzagging. She resembled a Mexican painter—or a Mexican painter's inspiration, with the exception of the brows.

But, before either of us said anything, I felt James had an unspoken moment with her. It was as if they shared a past, or, worse, a charming, fleeting glimpse of a future. Throughout our marriage, I would encounter this type of lady in numerous forms and guises. But she was simply a twitch in my tummy at the time.

Our next destination was Fred Leighton, a Mexican-import clothes store that had recently started selling fine jewellery. I was wanting to discover something practical and unique to wear at my wedding that I might possibly wear again in the future. I immediately selected the correct dress and held it up, secretly granting James veto authority.

When I remarked, "It's pretty loose-fitting, and it's a medium," he urged me to try it on. "It'll work," he said, "done!"

It was a basic grey-and-white long-sleeved Mexican garment, vertically striped and floor length, that reminded me of Lucy and my clothes when we played at the Moors in Provincetown. That dress—my wedding gown—is one of many articles of apparel that have inexplicably gone from my home, along with other treasured items. The lovely diamond necklace James bought for me after we married has also vanished. Countless pairs of my best, worn-in leather boots have also vanished throughout the years. Some of James's things have also vanished, including a lovely book given to him by Joni Mitchell that contained pen-and-ink drawings and handwritten lyrics to the songs on Blue, the majority of which were inspired by James. I recall Joni painting a girl's face with a sparkling diamond instead of a teardrop. My friend claimed she'd keep it safe for me.

* * *

I hung James's white linen suit in the shower to steam out the wrinkles after the plans were finalised. While I cleaned things around the flat and took David the dog for a walk, James napped.

I couldn't help but think of Daddy and how much he'd appreciate and approve of James. In spirit and manner, James was a Harvard boy who should never have gone to college. Ivy League or not, James was far too intelligent and perceptive for his own good. He moved around a lot as he slept, once telling me he'd dreamed he was emerging from a black hole, that he knew he wasn't from this world, but had no choice but to suffer the burden of life on this planet. I'm betting that 50% or more of James's thoughts or impressions were ones he wished weren't his. I thought he was an unusual talent at the time, and I still do.

That evening, however, James was nothing more than an anxious groom-to-be, and I was acting just as hard to be calm and unruffled, with both of us throwing aside traditional customs, including the wedding superstition of the bride and groom not meeting each other before the ceremony.

Our wedding style, if you can call it that, could be described as a slightly flamboyant lack of style. We didn't think the occasion deserved any hoopla or toys, paper hats, or long-winded, solemn speeches, and anything more than a low-key reading of our vows would have no sure dimmed James' reticently cheery disposition. We'd already had enough of a public life, one that would only become more visible and outspoken as time passed. We already had the usual number of people asking for autographs, James always signing his name with a quick "caged animal" scribbling, me offering a flawless schoolgirl script, making James's all the more valued. The attention people paid to us on the Vineyard at the time, and throughout the 1970s, would grow even more evident. James was drawn to the Lambert's Cove property because of its beauty and tranquillity, but neither of us had anticipated the presence of Cranberry Acres, a nearby camping site. Fans would come right up to the edge of our land and take pictures through the cabin windows. James would become enraged, but his road manager, Jock, would generally assist in keeping trespassers at bay. Things deteriorated over the decade, with automobiles cruising down our street at all hours, taking photos and movies, and some people even knocking on our door.

* * *

We stood beside the Tonk upright piano in our apartment, side by side, with James on my left, grasping James's hand and shaking from head to toe, with Judge Ash presiding. One of our unofficial ushers, James's (and now our) dog, David, was on the other side of us. In search of a distraction, my eyes were drawn to the camel colours on James' hand-painted tie. Oh my Lord, James, issues have arisen and will continue to emerge, but you are my entire life.

James and I both wanted the judge's address to be as concise as possible, with no religious references. His last words were: "Will you, James, take this woman, Carly, to be your lawful, wedded wife in sickness and in health, till death do you part?"

"Yes," James confirmed.

"And will you, Carly, take this man, James, to be your husband, in sickness and in health, till death do you part?"

I heard my own voice utter "Yes," while my brain took flapping flight, stumbling on far-flung trivia, as was its usual habit. Why and how did death you do part become death you do part? Where did you and what you did actually belong? Where did the adrenal glands exist in the human body? Were they at the back or on one side? But which side is it? Why was I still shaking so much, and where in my body was I feeling whatever it was, and how were my spleen and hypothalamus (wherever they were, though I thought they were fairly close to the adrenals) standing up under all this stress?

"I now pronounce you husband and wife…"

"You may kiss the bride…"

James and I kissed while Judge Ash retrieved a document from his folder. Then we did it again, and my mind was nearly bursting with Oh-my-god-Gods.

My mother was wiping away tears a few feet away from me. Having progressed beyond her initial assumption that James was a drug user (in the beginning, she referred to him as a "potter," not knowing exactly what "pot" had to do with drugs, or whether or not a verb or a noun was required), James now reminded her of Daddy in his younger days, back when she still loved him. In fact, as time passed, I began to suspect she had formed a crush on James, which was not really a stretch for my mother when it came to biblically inconvenient younger men. James, on the other hand, could "charm the ugly off an ape," as his own brother Alex described it.

When the gang left, I burst out laughing, euphoric, let-it-all-hang-out laughter that quickly evolved into weeping hysteria. My worried energy was infectious. James began laughing at me, and then at "it"—the entire ridiculous drama in which we'd just taken part, and the fact that he and I could now call each other "husband" and "wife" with perfectly straight faces. We stripped down to our underwear and headed directly to the fridge to retrieve the Sara Lee banana cake we'd purchased particularly for the occasion. Grabbing spoons, we both devoured the cake as if nothing we'd ever done, eaten, seen, heard, felt, or experienced had ever been so ridiculous: banana cake, for God's sake! We were like kids trying to loot the fridge before a responsible adult wearing a sheriff's star caught us. We ended up in the bedroom, resting on the carpet in a warm, worn nest of wedding gown, suit, camel toe, blue bra, stockings, pearls, and garter belt. We made love on the floor, gazing ahead as married people... or a couple of kids pretending to be married.

* * *

Love and marriage were one thing, but the demands of performance were quite another. On the night of our wedding, James changed into corduroys, work boots, a blue-patterned shirt under a Fair Isle sweater vest, and his now-familiar "lucky" turquoise belt. I wore a blue full-length cotton skirt, James's favourite item of clothing that I'd purchased in Greenwich Village right after graduating from Sarah Lawrence. It had the correct weight and length from the ground, with the waist allowing the top to bend down toward my navel like a bib. I completed my look with an Indian-made pink-cotton mirrored jersey from London that reached the top of my skirt, high socks, and clogs. We stepped out onto 35th Street and into a waiting stretch limo, considerably larger than we required and rather embarrassing in

James' and my shared reverse-snobbish sense. James went over the set list while the car drove uptown. He'd start with "Baby, It's Cold Outside," but when should he introduce me? He was trying not to pounce on himself for jitters; after all, that was my specialty.

The most important thing of all? We were both wearing our wedding rings. I kept looking down at mine, half excited, half sceptical. My ring felt like an amulet endowed with superpowers. Nothing can harm me anymore. I made things even more formal by changing the names on my three credit cards over the next four days. MRS. JAMES TAYLOR, DON'T FUCK WITH ME, would suddenly be emblazoned on my Bloomingdale's card. I'd never felt more certain of anything in my life as I did about my new marriage to James. I hoped, and could have sworn, that whatever anxieties, worries, and dark uncertainties I'd felt in the last year and before would melt to vapour and fade into the unseen ozone.

* * *

The after-concert party in the Time-Life Building was a rousing success. Every blood relative we had, as well as every record-company executive who had developed salable brands from our faces, bodies, and voices, surrounded James and me. Brothers, sisters, ex-girlfriends, ex-boyfriends, moms, and close friends (including a few smilers with knives) toasted us, as did Jac Holzman, Mo Ostin, Lenny Waronker, Peter Asher, and my manager Arlyne. I briefly considered Bianca's phone call the night before and rejected any importance it might have had. My family was there, looking slightly slighted at having been left out of the actual wedding ceremony—or maybe I was imagining things—and my brother Peter took photos, including one where James and I ate pasta, strands dripping from our forks over a shared plate, under the room's ghoulish overhead lighting.

I and James left early. As we boarded the elevator, other people flung rice at us, creating a grain-storm that slid down our shirts, into our hair, and into our eyes, though the majority of it ended up sleeting down the elevator shaft. Outside, it was chilly, and a mob of concertgoers approached James and me, begging for autographs. After cramming into the waiting limo, James and I jumped into each other's arms, half-screaming, "Hi baby, hi baby, oh God, I love you." We opened our apartment door ten minutes later to be greeted by David, who was looking guilty. While we were gone, David had burrowed his way into my lone clothes closet and chewed up all my shoes, rendering them useless as footwear but infinitely valuable as dog toys. The ones we carefully packed from the Barbizon were insufficient. David worked as a "shoe man."

I looked in the mirror as I was getting ready for bed. I wanted to bring everything together, not separate it. I desired to enter into a healthy union or a wonderful fourth with my darling. There was no trace of the Beast. The boys in the trees would now go. There was no reason to turn around and gaze at another man. I didn't feel the same way anymore. I no longer went by the same name. My professional name would remain Carly Simon, but if names are a form of music, my new name completed the original chord of "Carly Simon." I nearly felt destined to be known as Carly Simon Taylor from then on, the look of it melodious, balanced, a symphony of the spheres. Then there was my new husband, a man who made it easy to forget about my old self as the two of us pushed ahead, arms interlocked. I would ride the James Taylor train in sickness and in health for a very long time.

Chapter 12: Emulsification

Many marriages rise, collapse, and rise again. You say something inappropriate, reconcile, and continue on into the sunset. James and my marriage was like any other because, at the end of the day, marriage involves two people who need food to eat and a place to stay out of the snow, wind, rain, and too-hot August days, where they may bustle around, sleep, and rest their sore feet. The main distinction was that James and I were both entertainers, private individuals in the public eye. Blame it on that or our different personalities, but the waves and surf patterns that defined our marriage were, dare I say, bigger and more chaotic than in most marriages. Our love became bipolar, alternating between love and hatred, lust and loathing, and back again, sometimes within a single day. The pleasure with James was pure bliss, whilst the anguish was almost unbearable for me. Throughout it all, I was aware of my watchfulness, like a lighthouse keeper looking for signs that James loved me, that the two of us would be okay, that we would make it home safely. Because, no matter how many years pass, James will always be a huge part of what I call home for me.

These days, I'm worried that Ben and Sally, our two children, will feel their father is pleased with me. Obviously, not all of me, and not everything, but there was enough good in me, and in the two of us, that James would not want to forget me. I'm sure James remembers being in the delivery room when Sally and Ben were born, and that we bought and decorated a house on East Sixty-second Street, where we spent a few years while also jetting back and forth between the Vineyard and Los Angeles, before moving to a sprawling rental on Central Park West. Today, James would probably forget many of the things that I recall being flooded with colour, just as he would recall sunlight on days that I remember being dreary and dimly lit. Whatever he thinks of me today, I guess it's not as bad as the way I view myself through his distant eyes. I believe that even with the pacification of age and hindsight, he retains the right to thrash around in sullen revenge, a house specialty.

He might also recall coming home one night to explain that he'd spotted a girl from behind on the street and was completely captivated by the sight of her. He'd gone so far as to discreetly follow her for a few blocks, admitting that he felt horrible and uncomfortable the entire time. She, the girl, was tall and dressed in a hip-hugging leather miniskirt and chamois boots, and James was embarrassed to have lusty impulses for other women so soon after marrying. He then told me that the female had finally turned around. I was standing right there on the street. We burst out laughing into each other's arms.

James and I flew to Martha's Vineyard for Christmas a month after our wedding. A swarm of tradesmen filed in and out of our land, precisely as James, along with a motley crew of local carpenters and crafters, would do over the next five years on the house and surrounding fields. There were always workers hammering, sawing, cutting wood, building fences, clearing undergrowth, laying down pebbles, and constructing porches—"the circus that is my life," James used to call it. The kitchen wing was first, leading immediately upstairs to the bedroom. Workers were also busy planting, cleaning fields, and constructing stone walls, as well as a new, upgraded driveway. In the centre of the deck we were building, we planted a little kousa dogwood tree. As the months and years passed, the mere physical presence of so many beefy or skinny well-meaning tradespeople—along with the fact that James and I were rarely alone in our own house—began to irritate me. The incessant choral accompaniment of saws and hammers, however, was practically mixed in with the arrival of holiday parcels from Elektra and Warner Bros., reminding both James and myself how much our record labels loved and appreciated us. Most importantly, they were ecstatic about the growth of both our albums, No Secrets and One

Man Dog, which were climbing the charts and garnering a lot of positive press.

With our house absurdly cluttered and upturned, James and I piled into our equally cluttered car and drove over to Trudy Taylor's house for Christmas dinner, where we joined the rest of the Taylor clan. Despite my long, skin-deep relationship with some of James' family members, I was still the awkward newbie, but they were an astonishing collection of welcoming, energetic southerners, Trudy a lifelong Yankee, Like a southern-born one. Of course, I already knew Kate and Livingston—Liv is attractive, witty, and by far the friendliest of the Taylor children—but that night I also had the opportunity to speak with James's two other brothers, Hugh and Alex. Alex, the oldest, had a sonorous blues singer's voice that set him apart from the other Taylors, even the darling youngest, Hughie, who at seventeen was perhaps the "cutest" of them all. I drove home that night with the definite feeling that the Taylors, as a family, could be insular, engaged largely in the activities of its many members, with a collective tendency, one that James had honestly acquired, of rarely looking you in the eye. They were like an island tribe with a private, loving language that only they understood.

A new bride will inevitably begin to compare her new family to her original family of origin. With Mommy and Trudy living in Vineyard houses not far apart, I had the impression that Mommy was always competing with Trudy for the title of Best Mother in the Neighborhood. My sisters had always had a natural sibling rivalry, which was exacerbated by the fact that I was now married to a famous prince and receiving the royal treatment. The more that happened, the worse I felt and the more guilty I felt.

* * *

James and I had very little alone time that Christmas. The cabin in the woods—all four rooms of it now—was densely occupied with

Jimmy, Jimmy, John, Luke, and Laurie, the No Jets Construction Company, as well as a regular stream of visitors, some well-intentioned, some not so much. We took lengthy excursions through the nearly frozen woods on the next land to carve out some time for ourselves, stopping at an empty summerhouse to satiate our still burning newlywed urges. It was amazing, but not as easy as you'd think—staying in ecstasy while laughing our heads off as we made our way to a nearby residence. We never knew for sure if the house was empty, although most of the time it was. I was almost astounded at how much fun we had, getting down to our underwear and bending over washing machines, perching on couch armrests, positioning ourselves astride complete strangers' Shaker sideboards.

One day just after the New Year, Elektra called to say that "No Secrets " and its lead single, "You're So Vain," had both moved from number 39 to number one on the charts. It was a completely different experience for me, a performer in her mid-twenties who still considered herself as the stammering younger sister, the one who was always lagging behind. By chance, James's album One Man Dog and its lead song, "Don't Let Me Be Lonely Tonight," were released around the same time as mine. Despite the fact that James's new album was doing exceptionally well, it wasn't the monster hit that "You're So Vain" was turning out to be. You'd think I'd allow myself a few hours, if not days, of satisfaction or pride, but I couldn't. I had a love on the song "Don't Let Me Be Lonely Tonight," which was similar to my crush on James, and all I could think was that I wished it was him and not me.

It was the first time James and I had ever competed directly, and it perplexed me, not only because I'd always assumed James would be more commercially successful than me, but also because my desire to make him happy was so intricately woven into the submissive side I'd cultivated as a child by bringing Uncle Peter milkshakes with four-leaf clovers on top whenever he finished a tennis match. What is it about males that permits them to be comfortable as the successful ones, without feeling guilty if their women fall short? Like many women my age, I was horrified at the prospect of losing any rivalry with my partner.

Everyone else's brilliance paled in comparison to James', and I just hoped he could relish his own tone, poetry, and great virtuosity. To this day, "Little David," a song on One Man Dog, reminds me of my childhood Vineyard. I recall Davy Gude and David, our dog, and it all blurs and melts into then and now. In terms of my accomplishment with No Secrets, James couldn't have been more proud or gallant in complimenting my work, and he seemed to take genuine joy in the fact that he was married to me. When we picked up hitchhikers, which we did frequently, James always made a point of calling me by name in the car, adding a "Carly" here and there to let the individual know it was me in the passenger seat. But I could be wrong. I'd like to think he was pleased.

Simultaneously, I couldn't help but notice a fresh disturbance in the air. To make matters worse, my mother kept telling me that my sisters, Joey and Lucy, had both been individually ruined, like Anastasia and Drizella, after hearing the news about their stammering stepsister Cinderella, once best friends with cellar mice and dust balls, now riding around in magical style long after her midnight curfew should have expired. Instead of gloating, I was filled with guilt. It was stupid and wrong for me to come out ahead in the Simon family dynamic. Hopefully, it was only a fleeting concern.

Emulsification. I wasn't as knowledgeable about chemistry as James, who was genuinely interested in it. It was one of those words you'd heard but didn't know what it meant. I had a hunch it had to do with the breakdown of fat globules into smaller particles. The precise definition of the word wasn't important; what was important was that James, who had studied physics and chemistry, knew a term that I didn't and had pounced on me, humiliating me by purposefully making me feel stupid. He'd gone outside a few seconds later, leaving me bewildered, ashamed, and feeling bullied. Later, with the help of my dear friend Libby Titus, I compiled a list of other words and phrases that might catch me off guard in the future, such as détente, creosoted posts, and perestroika. Who knew what was going to happen next?

* * *

We flew to Japan in early January 1973, where James was on tour. The Japanese press seemed similarly enthralled by me, not to mention our marriage. Every night, one of the tour producers took the initiative to introduce everyone of James' band members who had arrived without a wife or partner to a Japanese woman of the night. It was a way of life there, just as it is for many musicians on the road, and the guys in the band loved travelling to Japan for that very reason, the ease with which the heart and the body could be separated. James and I spent three weeks in Japan, staying at the Tokyo Hilton despite his gigs in Osaka and elsewhere, and I couldn't help but wonder if he felt a little left out of the boys' club.

Another surprise awaited me on the Japanese tour. Almost every day, I received word from the lobby that a dozen red roses had been delivered to me downstairs. They were affixed to a letter signed M.P. Mick's alias was Michael Phillips, which he most likely used in hotel rooms around the world. What triggered this? I hadn't encouraged Mick, but I hadn't discouraged him either. He was aware that I was married, so why didn't I simply call him and tell him to stop? Any sensible female in a Jane Austen story would have done something like that. I believe Mick and I were both holding onto something, and I wasn't sure enough of myself to let go entirely. When James inquired where I got them, I lied and said they were a gift from the tour promoter for both of us. The roses kept appearing.

At the same time, the unexpected amount of attention that the

Japanese press was lavishing on James and me led to a painful but necessary honest chat about our rivalry one night. I'm not sure what we talked about, but it was about the massive popularity of "You're So Vain," the attention I was getting in Japan, and the idea that this might be one of the very few moments in my career when I was surfing a bigger wave than he was. James was conflicted about this, telling me that he didn't want to be jealous of or competing with the person he loved the most in the world. His statements were especially painful for me because I still felt guilty about being "big" or "important" in the Simon family. My mother had just chosen to leave me out of parts of her will because I wouldn't need the money any more. Worryingly, I never wanted to overshadow the man I adored. "What a good, if painful, talk it was," I wrote in my diary afterwards. "He did admit to me. He is really intelligent. I'm grateful for the opportunity to be so direct and genuine with each other. He never misses a beat."

* * *

Hallucinogens and other drugs were widely provided from record label presidents and A&R men to artists and their sidemen, backup vocalists, and stage workers in the early 1970s. Whatever you wanted was readily available: cocaine, mushrooms, LSD, marijuana, and a few new inventions just discovered in cutting-edge laboratories. That explains why one of the persons involved in the tour had lately given James and me four capsules of mescaline to take to Japan. (For the record, I was terrified of all psychedelics. People who knew me well, such as Jake and James, warned me that I wouldn't do well with them because my nervous system seemed to exist outside my body rather than within (or "in my plume," as my son Ben puts it), so I just stuffed the mescaline tablets into my cosmetics case and forgot about them. We didn't take them in Japan, and when we returned, I forgot about them, at least until James and I made a brief trip a few weeks later.

James's birthday, March 12, was quickly approaching, and I wanted to surprise him with a large, secret vacation where he had no idea where we were going. Despite my trip to Japan, I had developed an agoraphobia by that point. I'd never been the kind to venture far from the mother ship and the protection of my books and medicine cabinet, and it took a lot of courage for me to try a new restaurant. I finally decided on Bermuda, a two-and-a-half-hour flight from New York, and secured us a kingly suite at the Pink Beach Club, where my mother had stayed with Ronny and Peter after Daddy died.

When James was ultimately convinced that we weren't going to Bermuda for his birthday, but rather to a Cleveland tennis camp, he was noticeably unhappy. Nonetheless, I managed to pique his interest by purchasing not one, but two new pairs of tennis shoes, as well as top-of-the-line Wilson tennis racquets for both of us.

James had been on methadone for a year at that point, and he had packed enough doses to last him a week. Given that we'd be playing tennis indoors, we packed naively and wisely for cool midwestern weather. Then I got sneaky: I called the American Airlines ticket desk and asked the employee who answered the phone if she could change the name of our plane tickets to Cleveland, Ohio, which she consented to do. (Never underestimate the influence of celebrity.) "Just go to the first-class counter," she went on to say, "and I'll brief Rosemary there to keep your secret." Rosemary was, as promised, a model of prudence at the airport. We boarded the plane, stowed our bags, tennis racquets, and large leather hats in the overhead compartment, left our new, personalised Whitebook guitars with the attendant up front, and took seats in the third row. Thank God, not a single pair of shorts, sandals, or white pants hinted to our true location. However, once we were in the air, the captain shouted over the loudspeaker, "Good morning... Today's flight to Bermuda will take two hours and fifteen minutes..."

He asked James to open his luggage in a flowing West Indian accent, and after scrutinising the contents, he commented that James must be visiting Bermuda to take advantage of the island's abundant tennis facilities. Then he said, "I see you have a paper bag there." Would you mind letting me look inside? Oh, and what exactly is in those tiny bottles? Is it true that all seven contain the same liquid? Yes, methadone. And what is the purpose of that?"

The official scanned a letter from James' New York doctor detailing the cause for the week's supply, confirming with James that the drug was for a "mental situation." I was hearing this entire exchange in the next cubicle over, while partially undressing in front of a second customs agent, this one an attractive, middle-aged, no-nonsense woman whose name tag read CHLOE.

She opened my cosmetics case, which I hadn't unpacked or even touched since coming from Japan. It then dawned on me: those were the four dark-green mescaline caplets that had been provided to us. I may have mentioned them to James or alluded to them, but neither of us had touched them. The four pills were wrapped in a handkerchief and placed into a plastic travel-soap bottle. The quartet of caplets spilled onto the floor when Chloe opened the handkerchief.

Oh my god. What had she noticed in James's childish, birthday-boy eyes? My heart began to beat quickly. James and I had finished our celebratory vacation. We'd be locked up. Chloe's "little island safe in the sun" speech was no doubt one she'd given to any number of miscreants wanting to establish a fresh life here. James and I had made our decision, and on his birthday, no less. Deportation would be the best news we could get at this time, compared to whatever else was in store for us.

The end result was that James and I were free to go, but our medicines had to stay. We could go to our hotel, and customs would contact us once their inquiry was over.

We grabbed a cab to Tucker's Town's Pink Beach Club, which was slightly cloudy. It was about midafternoon. We changed into our tennis clothing (white pants and white shirts, as is customary at the Cleveland Professional School of Tennis) and headed to the courts. James was being a good sport for my sake, but while the two of us ate dinner in our room that night, I felt nervous.James was on the phone a few moments later, explaining that he'd made a mistake and that his wife still needed her medicines. In answer, the officer instructed him to ring the station's doorbell, and he would come down and personally deliver the 'erb.

It was a lovely and warm day in Bermuda, and after gaining instructions to Hamilton, James hopped on his bike and returned to the Pink Beach Club an hour later, armed with four pills of pure mescalito. He drank one of them with his morning orange juice, and while I didn't partake, I was content to accompany him. The rest of the day was spent going down the beach, reclining in the sun, and marvelling at individual grains of white sand. I'd wanted to take half a tablet, but with my temperament, I wasn't sure whether I'd be able to tell the difference between a good or even a poor trip and actual, wall-dissolving craziness. Regardless, it turned out to be one of the most pleasant days I can recall. James and I played cards that night before he tuned up his Whitebook guitar and started playing some island music.

I began dancing because I was reminded of some of the ukulele beats that Uncle Peter used to play for me when I was a child. "Do you remember the day your uncle taught us his dance?" James inquired.

He insisted on seeing the dance again. "Come on, sweetheart, you can do it." He turned up the volume on his guitar, his playing becoming more wild, which loosened me up. How beautiful and complete it had been for me to see my uncle Peter simultaneously singing and dancing, moving the lower half of his body like a motor gone crazy, his movements and motions belonging to an uninvented dance from a country on no world map whatsoever, his hands jabbing at his upper torso and face like some beatifically smiling Indian princess as his legs performed what I can only describe as the Monty Python version of an African boot dan. James and I were laughing so hard at the memory of Uncle Peter's dance that my face hurt. We skipped dinner that night and instead celebrated James's birthday in the bathtub, surrounded by candles, toasting Uncle Peter with flutes of champagne.

Congratulations, Simon Sister!

* * *

I discovered I was pregnant at the end of May 1973, after returning home from the most recent James tour. I'd travelled with James and his main band—Russ Kunkel, Lee Sklar, Danny Kortchmar, and Clarence McDonald—and when we returned to New York, I recall holding the news to myself until I was certain nothing untoward would happen. I slept around the clock for the first few months of my pregnancy, and James and I spent those dreamy months on the Vineyard, building the new "wing," its forty-five-foot-high tower the crown of the community. The wing contained a new living room space, as well as a true (albeit very small) kitchen adjacent to a central room with a brick fireplace and a dining room table with extra leaves for when we had guests. And there were always people there. I remember making large amounts of Trudy's clam chowder for the collected masses in the periods between sleeping and carpenters sanding the floors, surrounded by dusty people, many holding guitars, most smoking cannabis, all wearing swimming costumes. My own marijuana days had ended a few months before when a hash brownie nearly killed me. (At the time, there were no particular warnings regarding consuming marijuana while pregnant, though caution seemed to be the prevalent tone.) Dramamine was the only medication I used on occasion for sleep, seasickness, or airsickness.

When James and I travelled to Europe in July to meet two of our best friends, Ellen and Vieri Salvadori, he had just completed a two-week detox. Ellen and I had been friends since seventh school, and Vieri was my first partner in ballroom dance class. We were welcomed in Rome by a record industry official who took us to Siena, where Ellen and Vieri lived in a crazy lovely house overlooking what looked like a painting: Tuscan olive orchards amid a background of delightful, jagged, impossibly green hills. It was a very romantic scene, only James was practically untouchable, suffering from skin hypersensitivity if my leg even contacted him and denying all attempts at proximity or intimacy. "James just doesn't seem to want me," I jotted down in my diary. "I despise the bastard. Why do I adore him so much? Why do I dislike a Giver? I think I need enough enigminess to keep feeling as unworthy as I believe I am. Perhaps James has revealed his heart. To the opium. No, it's just me being overly needy."

James had been fairly chilly to me the entire trip, but when we arrived at the inn, he emerged from the toilet one night a shaved man. His moustache had vanished. It was a huge surprise: in our two and a half years together, I'd never seen him without one. (James had appeared without it on an album cover, but I'd never seen him without it in person.) He almost seemed embarrassed to reveal to me his face without his moustache, as if he'd never allowed me to see him naked before. He was immediately changed into the most bashful and fragile southern infant. Removing that strict Prussian-soldier barrier appeared to affect his personality as well, as all of his sweetness poured out, and after my period of feeling unwanted and missing being close to him, we made love like a pregnant wife would with her clean-shaven husband.

But I'd also realised James needed his space—physically and emotionally—and was likely to reject anyone who took away his raw square feet. If a close friend like Ellen Salvadori wanted a hug hello or a kiss goodbye, that was no problem, but a keen observer could clearly deduce that James was looking for the exit sign the entire time. This similar hypersensitivity to closeness, combined with James's coolness—if not outright revulsion—to anyone invading his bodily space, occurred after each and every one of his detoxes. He detoxed from methadone and opiates rather than alcohol. It became complicated, especially when he drank and the wine made him physically want me. Those nights were bittersweet for James.

We were both recording in Los Angeles by September of that year. I was working on my new album, Hotcakes, while James was working on his new album, Walking Man. Jake was also in L.A., living in Malibu, and he and I continued to work on songs, some of which we would save for future albums. Jake and I worked on a new song, "I Haven't Got Time for the Pain," in Jake's house, whose lyrics Jake penned right in the middle of recording the album. Jake originally intended it to be an

I-love-you-and-you-came-along-and-changed-everything song, but when I asked whether it was about Jennifer Salt, the woman in his life, he told me it was a Sufi song about Oscar, his Sufi master.

We were having one of the most relaxed marriages ever, with me pregnant and working and James composing and recording. We'd settled into a pleasant year and a half after a rough summer.

I'm generally euphoric and more in love with James; I'm not sure how it can continue. How much storage space do I have? It's fantastic. I am a romantic.

* * *

We had finished a new wing on the Vineyard house, as well as a few more sunlit terraces, by 1974, only to start dreaming other, future wings, carports, gardens, and—because I had too much idle, swimming-pool-construction time on my hands while James was on tour—a swimming pool. When James returned home, the pool was already full of water, with its edges encircled by filth, mud, and sand. It was extremely bold of me, and there was no justification for not walking James through it beforehand, even though I swear I did. (Judging by his reaction, I hadn't told him, but there was no way I would have gone ahead with such a major choice without first consulting him.) That was just one of the liberties I took that irritated him. Another was a year later, when I created a circular garden. That did not sit well with James. Both were bourgeois and selfish actions on my part, completely at odds with James's no-frills, cabin-in-the-woods New England mindset.

Mick once told me that whenever he needed to separate himself from me, he would recall the moment I told him I had a Swiss bank account. The only issue was that it wasn't true. I wouldn't have known what a Swiss bank account was in the early 1970s! It makes no difference. The point is that Mick was merely implying that I avoided being "bourgeois," and hence the polar opposite of what he stood for. That is to say, at least two key male role models in my life, James and Mick, had "labelled" me. Wasn't it Albert Grossman who said I'd be a perfect 10 if I didn't have money? The irony was that my father had been robbed, though I didn't realise it at the time, and there wasn't much money left in the Simon family coffers. When is this rich-girl image going to leave me alone?

Other disagreements between James and I included differing opinions on the proper colour for the trim on our now-expanded, increasingly imaginative cedar-shingled house. It was a fairly conspicuous structure by the mid-1970s, thanks to the 45-foot-high hexagonal tower James created, which soared up four stories. James chose yellow trim to make it appear sunny all the time through the windows, however I preferred a similarly cheery rosy pink tint. We reconciled our disputes amicably by counting the trim-worthy surfaces and dividing them in half, with each of us receiving an equal amount of paint. In the end, half of the trim was yellow and half was pink.

I knew that the press and those who loved us envisaged our lives on the Vineyard in a glossy, beachside mist, as a musical Camelot on the verge of a stormy, roaring sea, but our day-to-day life was far more mundane. People sawing and hammering on a house that seemed to never be finished, never cross the line of being "lived in." I was nearly always cooking. I became friends with several Vineyard hippie females, particularly Kate, Jeannie, and Brent Taylor, James's sister and sisters-in-law, with many of us pregnant at the same time, our aprons billowing white jobs over our swollen belly. At the same time, Kate was enjoying a very successful singing career.

The ordinary problems of two people in a very difficult profession were mixed together with home and domestic and pre-childbirth matters. James and I would frequently discuss our professional woes. One day he would console me, and the next he would be the one to console me. This show industry nonsense is for people who are egotistical enough to put themselves through horrible hardships for the odd ego fulfilment, I once wrote in my diary. Furthermore, the want for more attention, clicks, publicity, and triumph only grows. "It's great to have James as a mate—he's always understanding and comprehending every career situation," I said. He's wonderful. "I adore every hair on his head."

* * *

By November, James and I had moved out of the Murray Hill apartment and into a bigger place, a four-story brownstone on East Sixty-second Street, between Second and Third Avenues, where we would "live" for the next three years, despite spending the majority of our time in L.A. or the Vineyard. We had the first three storeys to ourselves, while the top story was rented out. New homes bring new faces and craftsmen, but I recall James being very husbandly and empathetic to me, his newly pregnant wife.

If there was ever a girl baby who didn't want to leave the womb, it was our Sarah Maria. She arrived three weeks late, and James and I spent almost the whole time with Dustin and Anne Hoffman. Dustin, I recall, had a plan: he would make me laugh so hard that I would go into labour. We passed the time by playing cards, eating hot Indian food in our brownstone, going to restaurants and shows—including a Peter Cook-Dudley Moore night on Broadway—and listening to Dustin read aloud from Lenny, which he was just starting to shoot. Dustin was desperate to induce my labour, but it turned out that the only time I wasn't trying—for Dustin's sake—was one night when I went to bed late. I recall the moon being closer to Earth that night than it had been in the previous twenty-three years. The night was cool and clear, and I had an unexpected thought: I should clean all the copper in the home. My water broke the next morning about 6:30 a.m. In a hurry, James summoned Lydia, our housekeeper and cook, and informed her that there was water everywhere.

Lydia wrapped two towels around my waist as James dashed down Sixty-second Street to call a cab. I'd had a bag packed for the entire month, and as Lydia wrapped my winter coat around my shoulders, all I had to do was pick it up and climb inside the cab next to James. It was January 7, 1974, and as we rushed toward the hospital, I felt as if we were driving right into the moon, which was still full and dazzling. James was beside me, doing his best to remain cool, though he made a point of keeping the towels around me at precisely the correct level to prevent a backseat flood.

Sarah, on the other hand, was going to take her time. She had different plans. She'd wrap her umbilical cord around her sweet little neck, and once we arrived at the hospital, I'd wind up pushing for seven hours with the help of Demerol. James and I had gone to a few childbearing classes together, where he learned a few techniques for what would be most helpful during the contraction stage, but they faded once my contractions began, because no one—no one—had told James to sit by my bedside, pretending to be a seagull flying high above the beach in Menemsha. Every time a contraction came through, James muttered, "Carly, Carly... the wave is coming in gently... Carly, just go with it... relax..." It was becoming increasingly difficult for me to relax, and I'd start screeching, but James's seagull-voice soared to match my level. "Carly, take a deep breath... The wave is approaching, gently breaking at the coast..."

"NOT AT ALL, BASTARD! IT'S NOT GOING TO STOP!" That was the best reaction I could think of.

But my seagull-husband was a master of improvisation. "All right, then, we'll go to the South Shore." We're here on Lucy Vincent Beach in Chilmark, and a monster wave is brewing. Oh, I should have packed my bird hat, the waves are crashing and the wind is howling..."

The pain was excruciating, which is not an unusual reaction. James asked the doctor to intervene, and the doctor did, admitting me to the hospital for a C-section. As the nurses fought to maintain control, there was a flurry of sounds ranging from muffled to metallic and clattering—probes, scissors, shots, towels. I heard James's voice, weak and birdlike, as if from another world: "Carly, see the seagull?" I'm flying over Niagara Falls... It's lovely... you'll be alright... "That's my girl..."

The doctor ordered scissors into the little operation area; a mask was placed over my face; and nitrous oxide was administered. As I was being counted, I heard James softly humming, "Bad, bad Leroy Brown... baddest man in the whole damn town..." Is he attempting to make me laugh? "Worse than old King Kong... meaner than a junkyard dog..." And then I held my lovely, golden, wonderful daughter in my arms. While waiting for Sally to arrive, James composed the complete song "Sarah Maria." Sally's birth meant everything to him, and he was an amazing parent to her while she was a newborn. That night, while I slept with my beautiful new daughter in my arms, James took a taxi to Trax, a New York nightclub, and sang the song to the audience: "Well, the moon is in the ocean, and the stars are in the sky, and all I can see is my sweet Maria's eyes, oh Sarah, Sarah Maria."

Chapter 13: Sheets that are the colour of fire

A year later, James and I were still together—somehow—and I was in Pittsburgh on a fourteen-show tour with my band. I was at an all-time low in terms of weight. I was shrivelled and terrified, and anyone who knew what a nervous wreck I was should never have let me leave the house, let alone perform.

The previous six months had been extremely difficult, beginning on the day a doctor informed James and me that Ben had been born with a "dysplastic kidney," which meant his kidney had been busily recycling pee back into his one-, two-, and three-year-old bodies. Ben had been unwell considerably more frequently than typical his entire life, and it wasn't until his grandfather, Ike, persuaded us to see a kidney expert that we discovered Ben had a congenital condition that surgery would thankfully be able to correct. We scheduled the procedure for early June.

Ben's relief was palpable when he emerged from surgery. Six months later, in a haze of sleep issues, stress-related weight loss, adult acne, concern, and anxieties, I was pressed to continue preparations for my approaching tour, attempting to connect with my band and forcing a smile onto my stuttering lips. After all, it's only fourteen shows, I kept telling myself. I kept pouring my really heavy emotions—my nerves, my completely lost feelings—onto the shoulders of my sweet lover, Scott Litt, the way James still had Evey or maybe someone else totally.

I'd also started writing songs, some of which were about James. Writing about my own husband was far more traumatic than writing about mysterious crushes. My approach was frequently moderately passive-aggressive, in the expectation that James would pick up on or learn something about how I felt, thereby avoiding an actual debate that would almost certainly end in a quarrel. Or, on occasion, my lyrics were clear and hopeful. I recall composing "James" in

1980 while he was asleep on the couch, completely trashed on something or other. "Your voice is like the water / when I lift the shell I can hear you pouring out your heart to me / James, the beauty of your voice fills me with sadness / James…"

As rehearsals began, I felt strangely disconnected and disembodied, a stranger to my own appearance and self. I struggled to read people's feelings for me or mine for them. Despite the epiphany in the mirror at Evey's, it seemed like I suddenly knew nothing about myself, including what I should wear and why, or how to style my hair, which looked just awful at the time, like a hayfield shorn by an eager, fluttering scythe. Internally, I felt equally imbalanced, as if my entire existence had been tuned to the wrong note, one that had been further warped by the high-pitched EQ of an early 1970s heavy-metal guitar, the lyrics on repeat: Ben. Sally. Sally, Sally, Sally. Oh, Lord, my dear James: I require your assistance. I can't continue without you. I want our marriage to be restored. I wish we could go back to the day we were born.

Everything was in order backstage at Pittsburgh's Stanley Theatre. Flowers in ultrabright yellow, orange, crimson, and even bright blue were everywhere, the latter very probably genetically enhanced to take on the rich, regal hues befitting a star. I felt like a gangster's girlfriend getting a withering bouquet of those artificial, food-dyed azure flowers. They immediately depressed me. Worse, Arlyne was not present that evening. No doubt she was tired of me—I'd been nothing but drama for her, and Arlyne, like most people, had her own drama to deal with—or perhaps she sensed I'd fail and shame us both. My darling sister, Lucy, had insisted on going to Pittsburgh and witnessing the event in person. She recognized how much I was hurting. She nabbed it.

Lucy had never seen one of my solo concerts before, not that there had been many over the years, just a few brief tours and numerous public appearances with James. Of course, the two of us had performed and toured as the Simon Sisters in our early years. I missed Lucy dearly when I struck out on my own. Lucy had always been my boss, the sister I knew would always look after me, since we were children. She had arrived in Pittsburgh tonight. Had she foreseen that she would have to look after me? Did she realise how serious the issue was? I have my doubts. I hadn't even realised it.

* * *

People continue to write to me with genuine compassion, claiming to have been there "that night in Pittsburgh," and their compassion never ceases to move me. That night, all of my efforts were focused on keeping my sanity. I was also really nervous, considerably more than usual. The contradiction, which I've faced numerous times throughout my performance career, was that performing allowed me to disconnect from myself, to dive into the love of the ten thousand people in the crowd, and ten thousand more waiting for the second concert. If only I could become lost in the rhythm of the music. The more I wanted the ecstasy of losing myself, the more losing myself seemed like drowning and awful dreams.

I went to my dressing room after a sound check and changed into a bright pink pantsuit made of thin, shimmering satin. It stuck to my bones, giving my knees the appearance of two identical medical reflex hammers. I also had no idea how physically weak I was until the show. An hour before I mounted the stage, I called home and spoke to Ben, Sally, and James, my three night-lights, whose radiance I knew would last forever, at least until their stars brought me back home. I wanted that reality like I needed Santa with all my might.

I recall thinking that if I didn't conquer this fear, I'd soon be restricted to my home, and just my home, and as the years passed, isolated in my bedroom, and finally, alone in my bed with a duvet over my head.

My opening act, a local Pittsburgh band, performed for 45 minutes. I heard clapping from the audience and took one last look at the mirrored wall, the phoney blue flowers beaming back at me. In my pink satin pantsuit, I looked fairly swank. Despite the fact that my bones were protruding, I was feeling well. My Valium had kicked in, and there was no reason to think my Pittsburgh gig would be anything out of the ordinary.

Did everything fall apart as a result of the previous year's stress? Ben? James? I've wondered over the years if I fell apart that night because Lucy was in the audience, and if I still felt terrible, so many years later, performing solo, as the headliner, without my elder sister at my side? I'm at a loss for words.

The audience was giddy when I first appeared, but why wasn't their energy and enthusiasm making me giddy in response? The set list began with "Come Upstairs," an uptempo song from my recent album of the same name, the musical beginning of which sounds like a whirling dervish group. If only... the song would have been vibrant, entertaining, and new. If only I could undo everything that had gone so horribly wrong.

When I started playing the tambourine for an eight-bar intro, my body started gyrating like James Brown, Mick Jagger, or a dervish. The first of numerous thudding heart palpitations began to seem like enormous steps over the dry landscape that was my chest. Turning away from the audience, I found myself facing Mike Mainieri, my musical and social director, who detected trouble—or, more likely, plain panic—on my face.

At least a hundred people took my remarks seriously, congregating in the front row, with the guards standing watch, eventually letting approximately fifty individuals to join a stage already crowded with musicians, amps, wires, and scrims. It was almost as if, after inviting my neighbours over for a spontaneous glass of holiday eggnog, the entire street had showed up, with little to do but circle a shaking, frozen performer whom some liked, some probably revered. Most sat on the stage's edge, as if I were a living, barely breathing funeral pyre, a woman writhing, crumbling, atomizing.

A small voice inside me told me to sing "De Bat," one of the songs from Boys in the Trees about carrying Sally home in my arms one night. That will cause you to lose yourself, I warned myself.

Good idea, bad timing. Nonetheless, I began singing and was able to animate the visuals by impersonating, or attempting to impersonate, the bodies of the bat and the cat.

As I waited for my heart to regain its usual beat, I hoped that "De Bat" would be just what the doctor ordered and get me back on track. Oh, how different things would have been if I could have surveyed the situation onstage from a great height, or even as a member of the audience. My brain launched a debate with itself, a series of unrhyming lyrics: "Hey, I'm doing fine. I'm making progress."

"No, you're not; did you just have that feeling?" That was a heart palpitation. You won't be around much longer."

"No—you can control it."

"This is hardwired, Carly." The phobic process is a self-feeding loop. You're screwed. You've always been that way. You will always be."

My adrenal glands were activated by the back-and-forth conversation. With my adrenaline flowing freely, my heart palpitations went into overdrive. Then there was the fact that I was bleeding from between my legs. What began as a barely discernible trickling drip soon transformed into a single blazing stream. My bed was on fire, as were the linens.

What was going on with me? My sister Lucy, along with a dozen or so audience members, had made their way onstage by this point.

They sat there caressing my ankles and feet. "Carl, you're doing great," Lucy said, and I couldn't help but wish she'd grab the mic and finish the rest of the show for me.

"I love that song," one fan commented, and she sang "De Bat" with me.

"I get anxiety attacks too," added another.

"Can we stay on stage with you even if you don't get better?" asked a third.

The fourth one said, "You have blood on your pants."

"I'm just going to run into the bathroom for a second, and I'll be right back," I began to address the audience in their seats, but most were roaring so loudly they couldn't hear me when I said it. As I exited the stage, handing my guitar to Lucy, the audience began to boo.

Why would anyone boo me after such an outpouring of love?

I had made a mistake. What sounded like booing was actually Don't go! Don't leave! I turned around after a few hesitation, and Lucy returned my weird stare. "It's okay, I have to stay," I said.

"Are you all right?" Lucy stated, though I had the impression she was masking deeper concerns. "It sounds great." I dashed to the restroom, sprayed cold water on my face, and returned to the stage in a heartbeat. The audience was overjoyed and grateful for their assistance.

I began to sing anything, anything, which was quickly followed by "You're So Vain" and "Anticipation." I was clutching my legs together. I still had no idea what was going on, but my chest palpitations were subsiding, allowing me to concentrate on a Kegel exercise, gripping strongly to reduce blood flow to a minimum. I'd gotten to the point where I didn't care if I lived or died. I kept looking over at Mike, who was nodding up and down in an exaggerated manner, as if assuring the audience—and me—that everything would be fine.

When I finished singing "Anticipation," the audience applauded me. Some fans were even standing in their seats or crowding the aisles in the hopes of swapping places with the fifty or so people onstage. The guards appeared to be less watchful than normal in keeping the peace, but they were at precisely the correct height and distance to observe where the blood had soaked into my jeans.

It wasn't long before it became evident where everyone's attention should be directed. Things became definite when a college-age boy, who had been patting my leg as if comforting an injured, scared child or animal, moved his hand away. Everyone in the band and the crowd could see at once that his hand and my two pant legs were covered in blood. I won't go into further depth. But I will say that if you can remember a night like that, it serves as a good barometer against which to judge the various highs and lows of your life.

Lucy's voice could be heard faintly: "We have to get you backstage."

"She's bleeding!!!" someone exclaimed, terrified. I was beyond stunned by this point, as Lucy, who was always and forever the boss, devised a plan and escorted me offstage behind the curtain, followed by Mike.

I popped a Valium. I had a shower. I took my temperature. I changed into jeans and a T-shirt and was back onstage in five minutes, moving like a hero in a sports movie, resuming my concert. As my arms found my instrument, the audience rose to their feet. When I sang "Legend in Your Own Time," ten thousand people stood and stayed standing for the next twenty minutes.

The ovations were long and numbing as I said good night. I wanted to believe and enjoy the clapping and cheers, but instead I was overtaken by annihilating humiliation. As I walked away from the stage, I considered the Beast and silently nodded. I knew it was up to something, but I didn't know what. I blacked out after falling onto the couch in my dressing room.

The second show of the evening was cancelled for obvious reasons. Lucy was adamant about it. I was simply too exhausted to perform. We cancelled the remaining six or seven tour dates. Unfortunately, the insurance companies did not pay the entire amount to repay the losses, which enraged the promoters, and despite the fact that I had a popular song at the time, "Jesse," the album, Come Upstairs, did not sell well.

* * *

Music, as always, was the only thing that could bring me back to life. But, at the request of my family, I checked into a general hospital before returning to the studio. I was now even lighter than I was before the Pittsburgh concert. Doctors examined my blood, glands, heart, and brain and advised me to stay under professional supervision until I could eat normally again. The terrible pressure of Ben's illness and operation, as well as James' and my splintering marriage, followed by the tragedy that was Pittsburgh, was too much for me to bear. So I lingered in the hospital for another month, and by the time I was released, James had moved on to another woman, Kathryn Walker, an actress who would later become his second wife. Scott paid me frequent visits, as did James, who once brought me a big bouquet of blue irises. I convinced myself that I wanted James to be with Kathryn, that he'd be better off with her than with me, and that I also wanted our relationship to be over—though that emotion lasted only a day or so. Still, I saw Scott, and the next two weeks were a haze of me gaining weight and fighting off various lawsuits from promoters who had never heard of the contractual phrase act of God, or if they had, were doing their best to declare themselves atheists.

In retrospect, James appeared to be more depressed—though not more anxious—than I was during our marriage, self-medicating his ailment with a wide range of specialist-ordered (and newly created) antidepressants, as well as alcohol and other inebriants. I diverted his attention away from my own nervousness by saying things like, "How 'bout a nice brisk walk on the beach?" If we did go, James would not even look at the water. I used to bribe him with food, music, or lovemaking when I didn't understand the condition of depression as well as I do now. Those were the times when I was most daring in front of him, singing, playing guitar, and even making music in an attempt to pull him back into the harmony and blend of life. I would talk in different accents, make up poems, and sometimes, when a lucky star shined down from above, James would give me a sideways glance of adoration. He'd pretend to get out of his depression by chasing me around the flat or tickling me. It was amazing how similar we were. Simply replacing masks.

James once warned me that I had a very poor threshold for any form of pain, especially psychic anguish, and he was correct. Antidepressants and other drugs have occasionally benefited me throughout the years. When they're working, I laugh and sing songs around the house; when I'm depressed, it's a completely different story. Home and family support me. My children assist me. That's why the end of James and my marriage was such a shock to my sense of wholeness. I never expected that our perspectives on divorce would be so dissimilar, that we would genuinely cease to be a family, and that it would be so terrible to me. When a marriage dissolves, you don't always get to choose what stays.

Chapter 14: Strip, Bitch

Nonetheless, things were hesitant until the end.

About a year after James and I divorced, he visited the apartment we'd shared on Central Park West, where I continued to live with Ben and Sally.

It was just before dinner time. James was dropping off the kids, who had just done their homework, at his new West End Avenue apartment. He came up with them, which was uncommon because he typically left them in the lobby. Wearing his heavy, faux-fur-collared coat, James approached the kitchen. He remained the tall ghost of the man I adored. In passing, he stated that a cab was waiting for him downstairs and that he was on his way to the Village for dinner.

During this time, our relationship was confused, sharp at times, and heated in hatred, with our visits and phone calls whirling with eloquent insults, like a lion and a lioness in winter. "Angry man, hungry woman," as James once put it. We were civil at other times. With a cab waiting downstairs, I imagined he'd just turn around and board the elevator again. Instead, once the kids had gone to their rooms, James sat in one of the kitchen chairs, facing me. As I leaned against the counter that night, I was wearing a suede, leopard-print wraparound dress. The dishwasher was on the dry cycle behind me, the steam pouring from its borders probably blurring and enticing my own edges—for a poor old southern baby in his cups (James was either drunk or stoned, or both), I may have been a sight for sore eyes. James stood two feet away from me, tipped over slightly at the waist, his left elbow resting on his left knee, staring at kitchen tiles he once knew well, a lighted Camel between his right thumb and index finger. One of his enormous boots' laces had fallen undone. He was still wearing his coat.

There was definitely tension in that room. My garment was filled with steam. The angle between James and me was jagged, odd in certain ways. A scream was about to erupt; a song was about to begin; and something was about to explode up. James' lips remained half-open after exhaling smoke, as if he'd become distracted and forgotten to close them. He'd stand up, give me a gentlemanly nod, open the kitchen door, and go without an insult, at least not tonight.

Instead, he raised his head. He was admitting to me. Normally, I was able to comprehend James' plethora of expressions. But I couldn't tonight. He shattered ash on the floor before flashing me two or three milliseconds of his faintly bloodshot baby blues. I realised he was perspiring.

"Strip, bitch."

James hadn't changed his posture as he breathed perfectly circular rings of smoke. He didn't blink, waiting to see whether I'd take his bait; I looked up, and he just watched me for a few seconds. I performed a quick, frantic inventory while looking up at the ceiling to break our eye contact. A few more seconds went by. From the kids' point of view, it wasn't out of the question that Mother and Father would disappear behind a closed door, where they could perhaps be having a chat, if not a disagreement. They could be discussing school timetables, pick-ups, and drop-offs. They could be pulling out their calendars and planning their vacations. It wasn't such an implausible scenario. After all, the bedroom where I currently slept alone was "our" bedroom not long before.

Under the overly bright overhead kitchen lights, neither of us had the time or motivation to do anything other than delete all judgement and be descendants of previous hominids. I'm not sure how we arrived in the bedroom or how I softly shut the door.

Time had passed, but there was nothing clumsy or embarrassing about what we did. We weren't quite fresh lovers; it had just felt like an eternity since he and I had shared the same nerve system. We were both silent and obvious. He forced himself into me, front of his body to my back. James's long, aristocratic fingers were stained with nicotine, I noted. I was mostly struck by the fact that he was not wearing a wedding ring. There was some hesitancy. But that familiar weight, like that of a sleek animal, clung to me. Later, I knew he'd apologise, that he hadn't meant to, that it didn't matter, but in those moments, I was in heaven that lust had brought him down. I imagined myself as Orpheus taking Eurydice out of the underworld, not daring to glance back until we were at least in the upper atmosphere.

But, according to the narrative, and despite the gender roles being reversed, I never glanced back, and James vanished.

* * *

Three years later, in 1984, I was introduced to Simon & Schuster's then-CEO, Richard Snyder, and his wife, Simon & Schuster president and publisher Joni Evans, at a dinner party on the Upper East Side. Dick and Joni were a New York power couple who tried everything they could to live up to, if not exceed, their reputations. After dinner, Dick turned to me and said that I needed to accompany Sally and Ben down to the publisher's new offices on 48th Street and Sixth Avenue. "Have you ever been there?" he said, and when I told him I hadn't, he suggested I go the next afternoon. "If you really mean it, I'll be there," I replied, adding that Sally and Ben got out of school at three forty-five, and would four fifteen work for him? Dick smiled, shuffled in his pointy shoes, mock-bowed, and said, "Okay, Carly Simon, I'd be delighted." Simply ask the receptionist to direct you to my office."

I clutched Ben, seven, and Sally, ten,'s hands as we poured out of the taxi and made our way into Simon & Schuster's dark, cavernous lobby the next day. I'd never given my kids any information on their grandfather, Dick Simon, how he'd once been the reigning king of publishing, how he'd established from nothing a company that has now become part of a massive media conglomerate with his incredible talent, innovativeness, and vision. Ben and Sally seemed to remember only that Daddy had met Albert Einstein—and wasn't Einstein the same person who discovered America?—and that Daddy's hairline had begun to recede when he was in his mid-twenties, and did that mean that I, their mommy, would go bald someday, too?

We three ascended the elevator to the top floor. It was difficult not to recall another elevator ride I'd taken in another building, in another decade, to meet Daddy alone on the twenty-ninth level. That was, however, twenty-five years ago. Unlike the previous Rockefeller Center elevator, this new one was smooth, faceless, and frictionless. It came to a gentle halt on the executive floors of Simon & Schuster. When the doors opened, I was startled and almost stopped in my tracks. My gaze was drawn to the names inscribed on the frosted-glass double doors: SIMON & SCHUSTER. As Sally's gaze met mine, I realised she'd just gained a fresh, slowly dawning understanding of who her grandfather had been.

We sat on navy blue leather seats arranged around an ultramodern, magazine-strewn table while we waited for Dick Snyder. Ben drew an action figure on a notebook while wearing his Lawrence of Arabia headpiece. Sally started working on a cat cradle. Still fidgety, she started unwrapping a piece of gum before my eyes gave her a small nudge. It's not the proper time.

I was in the midst of a career downturn in the volatile, up-and-down weather pattern that was show business at the time. When you're hot, you're hot, and when you're not, you're not, and I wasn't as good as I used to be at keeping my cool. I'd been moated off by the Camelot status of our marriage while married to James. People loved us, loathed us, frightened us, despised us, and surrounded us with jealousy, want, and need. They unlocked doors for us when we asked (which was almost never), eager to make their way inside this tall, strapping, lanky duo. For years, a near-mystical allure of power had protected, surrounded, and trailed after us, but now that James and I were no longer two against the world, I was in a state of temporary stagnation.

Naturally, I desired to be at the top once more—to feel connected, wanted, and adored. Knowing all too well the deception of show business, I should have been above status seeking, but I wasn't. In the end, the illusion of glitter and celebrity is just as powerful and pernicious as any other narcotic. You've been duped into thinking you want something you know is lousy, false, and transitory. The trouble is that it also makes you feel good, gives you a voice and an identity, and tricks you into thinking you are part of a higher tier of people who are more fun, sparkly, and worthwhile to be around. Most importantly, Hollywood makes you feel desirable, but with my marriage over and my career stagnant, I felt doubly unwanted.

* * *

Thirty minutes had elapsed. Then there were forty-five. Michael Korda, the editor in chief of Simon & Schuster, emerged in the corridor, and we chatted briefly before Korda was called into a meeting. While I waited for Dick Snyder, I informed my children about their grandfather's brilliance and risk-taking. Like mercury, which made Daddy mercurial by definition, an adjective that joined the word-of-the-day grammar list on our fridge, which included defenestration (the act of throwing someone or something out a window), lucubration (laborious, intensive study by lamplight), and pusillanimous (cowardly) that week alone. I informed Ben and Sally that Daddy was not only smart and personable, but he also had a famous reputation for developing and tending to his writers. He also never utilised fake praise. When he welcomed one of his authors with an eager grin or a hearty pat or clap on the back, he meant it.

The more I sat there, the more tense I became, my wallflower instincts fading and being replaced by fury. Dick Snyder was an hour and fifteen minutes late. I was starting to feel insulted and mistreated. My motivation for coming here was straightforward: I wanted to show Sally and Ben the company my father had started at the absurdly young age of twenty-five, hoping they'd be as proud of Daddy as I was. Just then, a receptionist led us from the reception area into another huge room devoid of all save a streamlined modern desk the size of a lap pool. Dick Snyder rose up and strutted across to the front of his desk, a Diet Coke can in his hand, peering down his Pinocchio-pointy nose at us.

I introduced Ben and Sally, noting that Ben's middle name was "Simon." Dick Snyder made eye contact and even shook Ben's small, solid hand in response. He seemed to notice Sally as he retreated behind his desk. He coughed into one palm before saying, "Sally, you said, yes—nice of you to come," and motioned for us to sit and make ourselves at home.

"Are either of your kids top students?" he inquired of Ben and Sally. "You want to come here and work some day?" Both youngsters nicely responded with "ums," with Ben even adding, "Yes, sir, I'd say so." Snyder described Simon & Schuster as a "pretty darn nice place to work." He smashed one final shot of his Diet Coke in one hand. Pulling his arm back, he fired it across the room into the wastebasket. He executed the shot with ease. A tough guy in a soft field. I couldn't care less, like Sally, but Ben was clearly impressed. Then, with the assurance of a slew of white boys in pin-striped suits, Dick Snyder looked down at Ben and Sally and said, boomingly, "Well, if your grandfather had been smart, this could have been yours."

* * *

Was this a case of history repeating itself? Was my existence, like

Daddy's, a gleaming surface under which the most heinous forces simmered and fumed? Had I spent my life trying to save my father, avenge the losses he had experienced, while yet doing everything I could to avoid becoming like him?

I, like everyone else, suffered losses, ranging from modest to major. Our family's unity has been our greatest loss during the last twenty years. Some fundamentals remain constant. My stammer continues to come and go, as does my stage nervousness. I still believe in the power of love entirely. I'd like to point out that defeats aren't wholly negative. Just as darkness follows day, misery follows joy, and the underworld occasionally targets innocence, a lifelong foe like my stammering turned out to be the same thing that made my music so important to me in the first place.

How can a person—me or anyone else?—move on, push forward in life? The answer is that none of us do, at least not completely. I've simply discovered a way to love despite whatever absences or disappointments have fallen like tree branches in my path. I proceed by absorbing whoever or whatever is absent or gone into my very being, my body, and my breath. This is what psychologists term introjection, but I call it surviving. I lost Daddy and absorbed him into myself. I divorced, and James became a part of how I viewed life. I let go of Orpheus, perhaps not recognizing that I only needed to get to know him before I could become him.

Printed in Dunstable, United Kingdom